By the Grace of God

By the Grace of God

A 9/11 Survivor's Story of Love, Hope, and Healing

Jean Potter

with Rob Kaplan

authorHOUSE®

AuthorHouse™
1663 Liberty Drive
Bloomington, IN 47403
www.authorhouse.com
Phone: 1-800-839-8640

© 2011 Jean Potter. All rights reserved.

No part of this book may be reproduced, stored in a retrieval system, or transmitted by any means without the written permission of the author.

First published by AuthorHouse   5/5/2011

ISBN: 978-1-4567-6605-4 (e)
ISBN: 978-1-4567-6607-8 (sc)
ISBN: 978-1-4567-6606-1 (hc)

Library of Congress Control Number: 2011906986

Printed in the United States of America

Any people depicted in stock imagery provided by Thinkstock are models, and such images are being used for illustrative purposes only. Certain stock imagery © Thinkstock.

This book is printed on acid-free paper.

Because of the dynamic nature of the Internet, any web addresses or links contained in this book may have changed since publication and may no longer be valid. The views expressed in this work are solely those of the author and do not necessarily reflect the views of the publisher, and the publisher hereby disclaims any responsibility for them.

A portion of the proceeds from the sale of this book are being donated to The Wounded Warrior Project and the FealGood Foundation

To
the 343 members of the Fire Department of New York
23 members of the New York Police Department
37 members of the Port Authority Police Department and all
the other innocent souls who perished on September 11, 2001
in
The World Trade Center
The Pentagon
Shanksville, Pennsylvania

CONTENTS

World Trade Center, September 11, 2001, 8:46 AM 1

Chapter One—Growing Up 3

Chapter Two—Jean and Dan 16

Chapter Three—September 11, 2001 25

Chapter Four—After the Deluge 49

Chapter Five—Battery Park to Bronxville 63

Chapter Six—Home in Pennsylvania 73

Chapter Seven—Survivors 84

Acknowledgments 93

"There is no center to this day, no middle or end. All its remaining minutes and hours will be collapsed into that single instant at 8:48 AM when September 11, 2001 became the saddest day of our history".

Dennis Smith, *Report from Ground Zero*

Fireman's Prayer

Almighty God, Protector of all Mankind, Your Strength, Power, and Wisdom are a beacon of light to all men and women:
Give special guidance to Firefighters so that they may be protected from harm while performing their duty:
Help them with your loving care while they work to save the lives and property of all people young and old:
Give them the courage, the alertness to protect their neighbors and all others whom they are pledged to aid when involved in fire or accident.

Amen

WORLD TRADE CENTER, SEPTEMBER 11, 2001, 8:46 AM

. . . all of a sudden, a thunderous explosion, louder than anything I had ever heard, ripped through the building. It was 8:46:30. I was thrown out of my chair as the building swayed from side to side several times. The air was immediately filled with smoke and a terrible smell that I didn't recognize. (It was only later that I learned it was jet fuel.) Tiles were falling from the ceiling, lights were swaying, and people were trying to regain their balance. I heard one of our associates yell, "Get to the staircase!" Of course, I knew immediately that something terrible had happened. Even so, the first thing that came to me was a voice saying, "This is not your time. We are with you. Your brother is with you." And I knew he was with Dan too. To this day, I don't know exactly whose voice I heard at that moment. It may have been my angel, or a guiding spirit. It may even have been Jesus. What I do know is that it was loud and clear. And that whoever it was, he was with us, those of us who would survive, as well as those of us who were passing over . . . .

CHAPTER ONE

Growing Up

With God all things are possible.
Matthew 19:26

It was only about a dozen miles from where I grew up in Brooklyn to the Bank of America offices in the North Tower of the World Trade Center. But when I think back on it now, it seems like I came a long way from where I started. Where I started was in Bensonhurst, a close-knit Brooklyn neighborhood that seemed to be made up half of Jewish families and half of Italian-American families. My family was one of the latter.

My great grandmother had come from Italy with my grandfather, leaving her other son behind with family members. She had an opportunity to come to America, and she seized it. Shortly after she arrived she purchased the house that I grew up in—a lovely four-family home with a very large backyard, not at all typical of the neighborhood. "Nonna," as we called her, lived in the front apartment on the first floor with my great grandfather, Nonna Orazio. She was the sentinel, the one who kept an eye on the neighborhood for all of us.

My family lived in the back apartment, and my mother's parents—"Nanny and Poppy"—and my Great Aunt Fran, my grandmother's sister, lived in the two upstairs apartments. The apartments were relatively small, but the basement could easily accommodate large gatherings. That's where everyone got together for holidays, which was very typical in Italian-American households.

I have very fond memories of my childhood, always surrounded by the family's love, particularly my Nanny's. I remember that she would often call down from the second floor, "Jeanna, I just made *merluzza* and *broccoli di rape* for you." My two all-time favorites! *Merluzza* is whiting, and Nanny would make a cold fish salad with olive oil, lemon juice, and fresh parsley. She would also painstakingly pick out all of the bones. And fresh *broccoli di rape*, with garlic and olive oil! I can still taste it today! My brother, John, and I also had the run of the house. Upstairs, downstairs, in and out of everyone's apartment—the doors were always open, and we were always greeted with hugs and kisses. Uncle Frank, my mother's brother, played with us—board games, card games, outdoor sports—and took us bicycle riding, and Aunt Grace, my mom's sister, would take us shopping for toys.

When I had to buy holiday dresses, though, it was Nanny who would come shopping with us. She was the head draper—that is, she would pin and drape garments on models—for Adele Simpson, the designer who dressed most of the country's First Ladies at the time. My Aunt Fran was in the clothing business too—she was a fancy sample maker. That's why my mom always had the most gorgeous outfits for special occasions. Perhaps that is where I got my appreciation for beautiful classic clothing. Even more important, all of these women were strong female role models for me as I was growing up. My Nanny and Aunt Fran trekked to Manhattan every day for work, and Nonna had a job doing all of the specialty hand sewing on coats in a factory in Brooklyn. My mom helped Nanny prepare all the meals, or at least she did until my brother and I were in school. Then she started working part-time as a bookkeeper. These were strong, determined women who "brought home the bacon and could fry it up in a pan."

Poppy managed the Nedick's in Times Square, one of a chain of cafeteria-style restaurants with counters where you could get a simple meal. They were famous for their hot dogs and orangeade. In those days Times Square wasn't what it is today. It was a pretty rough area, with unsavory characters and porn theaters all over. But even unsavory characters needed a place to grab a quick bite, and Nedick's was it. Sometimes Poppy would take us to work with him on a Sunday, and it was fun. He was a wild man running that place. One summer my Uncle Frank, a youngster at the time, went to work at Nedick's, and Poppy would scream at him if he sat down even for a second. We still laugh at those stories.

It was my Nanny, though, who was my dearest friend. As a teenager, when I stayed at home while my parents went upstate to their country home on weekends, I would start my day off upstairs having coffee with her, discussing everything under the sun. How I loved my Nanny. She was always there with her beautiful smiling face and tender ways. Everyone loved my grandmother. Growing up, every Sunday we would all gather upstairs for a beautiful Italian meal. You would begin to smell the meatballs frying and the sauce cooking from early in the morning. When my sweet Nanny passed after a long battle with breast cancer,

I was heartbroken and found it very difficult to walk into that apartment, especially the kitchen where we would share our lives and hearts. My grandfather always ate with my parents so I would see him, but I rarely went upstairs anymore.

At Nanny's wake, the back of her prayer card read:

To Those I Love

When I am gone, release me, let me go.
I have so many things to see and do.
You mustn't tie yourself to me with tears,
be happy that we had so many years.
I gave you my love.
You can only guess how much you gave me
in happiness.
But now it's time I traveled on alone.
So grieve awhile for me if grieve you must,
then let your grief be comforted by trust.
It's only for a while that we must part,
so bless the memories within your heart.
I won't be far away, for life goes on,
so if you need me, call and I will come.
Though you can't see or touch me, I'll be near,
and if you listen with your heart, you'll hear
all of my love around you soft and clear.
And then, when you must come this way alone,
I'll greet you with a smile, and say "Welcome Home."

Like my mother's parents, my dad's parents, Maria and John Gammone, had come from Italy to America so they and their children could have a better life. Grandpa would often tell us how they couldn't wait to come to America, because the streets were paved with gold. He and my grandmother, another wonderful role model, felt very privileged to be in this great country. Visiting them on Sundays was always joyful, even when Grandpa would pinch my cheeks so hard they would hurt! I still think very often of Grandpa, who loved walnuts and black coffee, and Grandma, a beautiful, statuesque, sweet woman who always had a smile on her face. For some reason, I particularly remember how one day she made "flowers" for me for to eat—zucchini flowers—and they were delicious!

Grandpa Gammone was a barber, and my father and his brother, Uncle Albert, worked with him in his shop in Brooklyn. But one day in 1969 my dad decided to take a test to be a meat and food inspector for New York State's Department of Agriculture and Markets. He passed with flying colors and began his employment with the department. He worked there until 1975, when he became an import inspector with the United States Department of Agriculture's Animal and Plant Health Inspection Service. He thoroughly enjoyed his job, and was very well suited to be "Inspector Gammone." He retired in 1992.

My dad's mother, Grandma Gammone, passed away in 1971. It was right before Christmas—I remember waiting to go to the funeral parlor as they were about to light the tree in Rockefeller Center. To this day I recall that moment whenever they light the tree. I felt my grandfather's pain deeply as he cried out her name, "Maria, Maria, Maria," over and over again. A member of the family recently found this poem, which my grandfather wrote after my grandmother passed. We all cry whenever we listen to these beautiful, profound words of love and devotion:

Maria Mia

> You are the owner of my world, rich and
> poor I am for you
> Like the earth, sky and ocean forever all
> around you
> What courage you had to break this love
> without a reason
> I don't see her anymore
> Oh, I loved her so much, she was my life
> She carried a beautiful name
> Maria Mia
> Our love was one soul and then your destiny
> broke it
> These words, bittersweet and burning,
> passionate to save you
> But you, cruel destiny, you stole her from my
> arms
> How badly you hurt this heart of mine
> Oh, I loved her so much, she was my life
> She carried a beautiful name
> Maria Mia
> I shed tears and sighs continuously,
> emblazoned in my heart
> I remain, never forgetting her touch
> She was my life
> She carried a beautiful name
> Maria Mia, Maria Mia, Maria Mia, Maria
> Mia, Maria

What a love story theirs was . . .

As you can see, I am very proud of my heritage, and indebted to my wonderful family for all of the values they instilled in me.

ONE OF THE VALUES MY parents gave me was a strong work ethic. Even when I was a teenager I always worked part-time. I loved earning my own money, and spending it! On weekends my girlfriends and I would often take the train from Bensonhurst to Greenwich Village to go shopping. Eighth Street was the Mecca for all things wonderful—shoes, clothing, leather goods. We loved doing that. The city was always my playground, even from a very young age. But I always worked very hard. As a young teenager I would baby sit the local children when their parents needed a break and wanted to see a movie. I also worked part-time in the local dry cleaners every summer and on weekends when school was in session. I loved to work. I guess it's a Capricorn thing.

When I was in high school I started working part-time in Manhattan during the summer. My first job was with the Jewish Child Care Association. I worked with the sweetest older gentleman, who smoked a cigar and called me "sweetie" in a thick European accent. He was wonderful, so wonderful that I came to love the smell of his cigar. The association offered me a full-time position when I graduated, and as soon as school was over, it was off to work I went. I must say that my guidance counselors were terribly upset that I wasn't going to college, as my grades were always excellent, and I did love school. But I really wanted to work, and at that point in time you could get by with a high school education. Today it's a much different story. If I had gone to college, I probably would have majored in medicine, because I loved science. But I really have no regrets. I had an excellent career as an executive assistant, and I made a decent living. Who knows, perhaps I'll go back to school one day.

Working at the Jewish Child Care Association was a wonderful way to start my career, and I really enjoyed working there. When I left the association, I went to work for a wealthy gentleman in his Sutton Place apartment. He wasn't married, and I was responsible for managing his finances and running the household staff. He was a serious collector of artwork, jewelry, and ancient artifacts, and I would often be on the phone with auction houses. On occasion he would dump thousands of dollars in cash on my desk and say "Jean darling, would you count this and put it in the various household funds"—amazing! He had two beautiful kitty-cats who would help me daily. One sat on the desk, and the other on my chair right next to me. It was an interesting position—the job, that is—but I eventually left because I felt I needed to be in an environment with more people.

My next job was as executive assistant to the president of Calvin Klein Menswear. That was fun—it was almost like the movie industry. There was lots of hard work, but it was fun setting up fashion shows, working with Calvin Klein and his assistants, as well as with the sales staff. I also always had fabulous Calvin Klein clothing, because that's what we had to wear in the showroom. After a few years, though, I left to work as assistant to Joe Gargan, the vice president of sales at Elizabeth Arden. It was while I was working there, in October 1983, that I married Vincent. Vincent was a lovely gentleman, but ours was not, I'm afraid, a match made in heaven. Over the years we grew apart, and we were divorced in 1994.

When I left Elizabeth Arden I went to work as executive assistant to the chief financial officer of Revlon, Bill Frank. Bill and I interacted daily with Ronald Perelman, then, as now, chairman of the board, and his staff. Bill generally traveled back and forth to the West Coast every other week for a day or so. Every so often he would get stuck in traffic on the way to the airport and he would call me up and say, "Jean, would you call the gate for me please?" I would call the airport and tell them that Mr. Frank would be there momentarily and ask them to hold the plane. And they would say, "Of course, no problem." (Somehow, I don't think we'd be able to do this today!)

It was my job at Revlon that enabled me to get my apartment in Battery Park City. I was recently divorced and wanted to move out of the coop where I was living in Brooklyn. One of my coworkers told me that her boss had an empty apartment in Battery Park City that he and his wife were willing to rent out. They had built a beautiful home in Briarcliff Manor, in Westchester County, but wanted to keep their apartment in the city, even though they had no intention of using it for a long time. So I took the keys and went to look at it. The minute I walked into that apartment I knew it was home, and it was my home for nine years. When I told my parents I was moving to Manhattan they were very nervous about it until they saw where I was going to live. They loved it too. Home sweet home. I always felt so safe living there, safe and so comfortable, and it was a wonderful feeling.

Up to this point my career had been in fashion and cosmetics. But then changes started taking place in Revlon's upper management, and I decided it would be a good time to look elsewhere for a job, this time in the financial industry. My first job in that field was with Arni Amster, a private investor, managing his office and his financial affairs until he retired. I then went to work for Larry Fink, the chief executive officer of BlackRock Financial. It was while I was working for Larry that, on May 17, 1999, my sweet brother, John, passed.

John had gotten off the path a bit. Drug use had ravaged his body and his soul. I knew the time was nearing for him to leave the earthly plane. That particular day, though, I was in a total "flow" at work and I didn't feel him leaving us. It wasn't until I got home from work that I received a phone call from my dad saying, "John is gone." It was heartbreaking. I was completely devastated. He was only forty-two years old. You see your parents aging and know that they will pass before you do, but you never, ever think that you are going to lose a sibling. I can't express how horrible it was. I felt completely disconnected from "earth"—like an astronaut in space connected only by a thin lifeline. John was one of the most wonderful human beings you could ever meet. He touched the lives of all those he encountered, and always made things better and more comfortable for everyone around him. He was very handsome, with dark brown hair and big beautiful brown eyes. I can still hear him say, "Jean." I often hear his voice in my ear. I miss him so. He took a piece of my heart with him when he left that day, even though I know he is always around me.

Because of the debilitating grief I felt at John's loss, I decided to seek a position that would be a little less stressful. That's how I ended up being interviewed for a job as executive assistant to Lou Terlizzi, managing director of Deutsche Bank. LT and I hit it off right away, and I was offered the job immediately. The bank's offices were then located in midtown, but they were being relocated to lower Manhattan later in the year. I wanted to work downtown because I had spent my entire career working in midtown, and I thought being downtown would be a nice change. I'd even be able to walk to work, because Deutsche Bank was going to be located on Liberty Street. I accepted the offer and became part of LT's team.

There were several other individuals who had worked for him at other firms and followed him to Deutsche Bank. I soon found out why. LT was always loyal to his employees and generous to a fault with family, friends, and associates. His beautiful wife, Debbie, and their three children—Danny, Ellen, and Gracie—are the apple of his eye. I can still recall a phone conversation I had with him many years ago when he was on vacation. He and Gracie, his youngest, were fishing on a pier, and as I held on the phone, waiting to discuss some important matters with him, I could hear him telling Gracie exactly how to bait the hook and fish. It was so endearing. That moment has always stayed with me.

In the fall of 2000 LT left Deutsche Bank to become managing director at Bank of America. I went along with him, as did, several months later, some of the others who had followed him from other firms. When we started there, we were on a lower floor in the North Tower of the World Trade Center. But in July 2001 we all moved up to newly-built offices on the eighty-first floor. You had to take two elevators to get to eighty-one. The first was an express elevator that went to a "Sky Lobby" on seventy-eight, and the second was a local elevator to eighty-one. Getting up to the office could take a few minutes, especially if there were a lot of people waiting for the local elevator. I must admit those elevators always made me a little nervous. When I got on to the first, I'd take a deep breath, think of my sweet brother, John, being with me, and up we'd go. It was quite a ride!

Our workspace on eighty-one was truly magnificent. Our offices took up the whole floor with the exception of two or three smaller firms located outside of our space. It was an open floor plan with offices and conference rooms around the perimeter of the building. Of course, everything was brand new. The furniture and cabinets were a beige/gray, very soothing, and they were arranged in rows to separate the different areas. We had a very large comfortable kitchen area with a table, refrigerator, vending machines, just about anything you'd want. It was like a home away from home.

LT's office was in the northeast corner of the building, and I had my own cubicle right next to it. Needless to say, the views were amazing. We could see weather patterns and storms coming in. Sometimes there were even helicopters flying lower than our windows. I often felt like I was in an airplane. There was one thing, though, that was a tad creepy. We could often hear the building sway. Yes, it swayed. But it was built to sway. If you stood by a window and held a pencil straight up in front of it you could even "see" it sway. Even so, I always had a very peaceful feeling being there. Being up in the sky, away from the noise and everyday chatter of New York City, was almost heaven-like. It was quite magical.

I would usually start my day between seven and eight o'clock in the morning. LT was always in early. At around nine, when everything was up-to-speed, I would often run down to the concourse to do some quick banking or errands and pick up LT's favorite coffee. The concourse was so terrific. It had every shop, service, and restaurant imaginable. Whatever you needed—from a tube of toothpaste to a pair of designer shoes—was all within a few feet of each other. Most of my day, though, was devoted to taking care of Lou and his staff. Keeping the work moving, e-mails going out, and following up when needed. And I worked with a great group of people. LT was the greatest boss, and his staff was a very tightly-knit group. It was like family. Yes, this was truly a job made in heaven.

CHAPTER TWO

Jean and Dan

God be merciful unto us, and bless us;
and cause his face to shine upon us.
Psalms 67.1

IN THE SUMMER OF 1997, when I was still working for Arni Amster, I had been divorced for almost three years. I had dated some, most of my dates being "corporate" types, but I still hadn't found my soul mate. Dating is never fun at any age, but it's a nightmare when you have been married before. And I was finding it all really difficult. I never went to bars, my close girlfriends were all married, and it was hard to meet people. I spent many Saturday evenings by myself rather than go out just for the sake of having dinner with someone. Yes, I was very fussy, but I felt I had a right to be. That's what made me look into the personal ads.

Late in June I answered an ad from a man who said he was a New York City fireman who was separated from his wife, and described himself as "romantic" and "sincere." I was very skeptical about all of this, but I was able to work up the courage to answer the ad—one of the first ones that I answered—and we made a date for July 5. I was excited at the prospect of meeting him, but I was terribly nervous all day. I needn't have been. When I walked into Martins BBQ, a restaurant in Tribeca, I was greeted by a very tall, handsome, soft-spoken gentleman. I remember that I was somewhat relieved when he opened his wallet to show me photos of his children, and I saw his FDNY shield. "At least," I thought, "he really is a fireman." We chatted for a while. He ordered a scotch on the rocks, and I had water. It was a nice evening. We walked through Greenwich Village, and he told me that he and his wife had only recently separated. Normally, hearing that would have made me "run for the hills," because I never wanted to be in the middle of someone else's divorce proceedings. But God had another plan.

We began dating. On our second date we had dinner at Walker's, another restaurant in Tribeca, and on our third date we played pool in Soho. Our feelings for each other grew quickly. It wasn't easy, though, because Dan's divorce was very problematic. He had financial issues, as well as issues with his children. It was a bumpy ride, and I did all I could to support him. In the meantime, he learned a lot about me and I learned a lot about him.

I LEARNED, FOR EXAMPLE, THAT Dan had a typical suburban Long Island upbringing. He was born in the Canarsie section of Brooklyn, and his parents moved to Brentwood, further out on Long Island, soon after his birth. At the time, it was a new development with lots of children to play with, and he loved it. Dan, his younger sister, Stacey, and his two brothers, Mike and Tim, would play ball and ride their bikes for hours. But even at the tender age of eleven Dan knew he wanted to be a fireman. He made the decision when he was at his grandmother's wake in 1968, when he witnessed two fire trucks in Brooklyn, a Ladder and an Engine, responding to a scene, and he thought, "That's for me." And from that day forward being a fireman was always in the back of his mind.

When he was thirteen years old he saw an article in a magazine about someone who collected fire equipment, and he decided to start his own collection. The postman who delivered his mail was the chief of Brentwood's volunteer Fire Department, and when he saw all the fire department mail coming in he told Dan that Brentwood was going to start a Junior Fire Department. That was music to Dan's ears, and he became a Junior Firefighter. Then Jack Mayne, Dan's father's friend, who was in the FDNY, learned about Dan's interest, and invited Dan to his firehouse, Engine 82/ Ladder 31, in the Bronx. Soon after that, Jack brought Dan to a fire scene, and let him ride back to the firehouse in the front seat of the ladder truck. Dan was hooked! After that, Jack often took Dan to the firehouse, and it was there that he met Mel Hazel. They hit it off immediately, and Mel befriended Dan. Mel often came in on his day off to show Dan the ropes of being a fireman. Mel truly personifies the brotherhood of the FDNY, and Dan feels very lucky to have had Mel as a mentor and as a friend.

Dan's father, though, had other plans for his son. An electrician by trade, he tried to teach Dan electrical work. He even set up a board with some electrical connections for Dan to practice on. But Dan wanted no part of becoming an electrician. He really wanted to be a firefighter with the FDNY. His father, recognizing that Dan wasn't going to be deterred, advised him to not "put all his eggs in one basket." Taking his father's advice, at the age of seventeen

Dan began writing to major city fire departments to take their local exams. He and three of his friends—Phil Buffa, Bob McClaferty, and Mike Morris—took tests in Anne Arundel County, Maryland; New Haven and Stamford, Connecticut; Cleveland, Ohio; and Washington, DC, as well as in New York City.

He was called for New Haven, but he was too young at the time. Even so, the fire chief was so impressed with Dan that he wrote a letter of reference for him. Dan was also the fifth person eligible to be hired in the Anne Arundel test, but was too young for their department too. It was Washington, DC that hired him first, at the age of twenty-two, on August 6, 1979. So he and his new wife—he'd been married the year before, moved to Washington, where they would spend the next three years. It was a remarkable time in history, and he thoroughly enjoyed his fire duty in DC. It was the end of the Carter administration and the beginning of Ronald Reagan's. The hostages came back from Iran, for which Dan was involved in security. There was a plane crash on the Fourteenth Street Bridge, and President Reagan was shot. It was a busy, active, history-making time.

But Dan had always wanted to work as a fireman with the FDNY, and he got his wish when he was hired on August 6, 1982, and was sworn in the following day. Both Jack Mayne and Mel Hazel provided references for him. He began working at Engine 88/Ladder 38 in the Belmont section of the Bronx. He worked under the close supervision of Captain Timmy Gallagher, who taught Dan the real nuances of firefighting. Captain Gallagher ("Tough Timmy") was a scrappy, aggressive, no-nonsense boss. He was a tremendous influence on Dan, and really prepared him to be an excellent firefighter. Dan worked in Engine 88 for four years, then transferred to Ladder 38, working under Jack Mayne, who was the company's lieutenant.

Dan was at Ladder 38 for two years, which is where he met Brian Hickey, who had recently transferred from Harlem. They became fast friends, and often compared notes regarding their careers. In 1989, though, they both decided it was time for them to move on. Dan transferred to Ladder 112 in Bushwick, Brooklyn, and Brian to Rescue 4 in Queens. Being at Ladder 112 required all of the firefighting skills and experience Dan had. Because there were a lot of tenement, wood-frame, and brownstone houses in the neighborhood, it was one of the busiest fire companies in the city at the time. Dan was there for six years. At that point in time he moved his wife and two children from Long Island to upstate New York, and transferred to Ladder 5 in Greenwich Village, right after the Watts Street fire that killed three of its members.

It was at Ladder 5 that he met Lt. Mike Warchola and Lt. Vinny Giammona, his bosses, who would later become his close friends. But after about six months he wanted to leave Ladder 5. He enjoyed the rescue work, but he missed going to fires, and wanted to transfer to a company with more fire duty. Mike Warchola, with the captain's permission, offered Dan the chauffeur's seat on Ladder 5 to keep him from transferring. The chauffeur's seat is a very prestigious position. Dan would, in addition to his fire duty, drive his bosses to the scene on the ladder truck. He accepted the job, and would be at Ladder 5 for seven years. In fact, that's where he was working when we first met.

Dan and I had been dating for a little over two years when, on August 6, 1999, I took him out to dinner at one of our favorite restaurants, The Hudson River Club. I thought we were celebrating his "FDNY Anniversary." But when we got to the restaurant, they seated us at a table with six place settings. I got a little annoyed, and asked why they were putting us there. When they explained that there were no small tables available, I asked them if they could please "unset" the table so there would be place settings for just the two of us. (They were probably pretty annoyed, but they never showed it.) They reset the table, and Dan and I sat down. About two minutes later, he said to me, "I believe we have turned another page. Would you marry me?" and presented me with a gorgeous diamond ring. Through the tears I managed to say "Yes," and all of a sudden I saw my parents and his parents walking over toward our table to join us. They were all in on it. In fact, the diamond in the ring was from my mother's engagement ring. And, yes, the waiters had to reset the table again!

Early in December Dan moved into my apartment in Battery Park City, and on December 12, 1999, we were married. Battery Park City was really unique. Our building was directly on the Hudson River, but our apartment faced the World Trade Center. The staff of the building was like family. By that time, I had lived there for seven years, and I loved the concierge, the doormen, the super, and all the wonderful staff. Whatever we needed, they took care of it. It was so beautiful and quiet that I always felt like I was on vacation. In the summer I could hear the sound of boats and jet skis racing on the Hudson River. We would often sit on a bench in Battery Park, the same bench on which Dan would be photographed after the attack on the World Trade Center, and watch the world go by, discuss our day, our plans, and everything else under the sun. Winters were peaceful and serene. And in the concourse underneath the Towers, a two-minute walk from home, were all of my favorite shops—from Ann Taylor to Sephora to Borders, fabulous restaurants, you name it. Even on the coldest days of winter all we had to do was cross the street and we would be in the concourse having fun. We loved living there.

One of the best things about being married to Dan was getting to know his son, Craig. Although there had been difficulties between father and son when Dan and his wife first separated, by the time I came into the picture they had developed a very good relationship. And because of that relationship, Craig has always spent a lot of time with us, especially when we lived in Manhattan. In fact, he grew up right before my eyes. When I first met him, in January 1998, at a birthday celebration for Dan's sister, Stacey, he was just about to turn eighteen. And now he's a fine young man, sensitive and caring. Craig is all about family. We have a very strong connection—I can think of him, the phone will ring, and it will be him on the line. We share so much, and I feel blessed to have this relationship. I have the best stepson in the whole wide world. He is an Iraq war veteran, and a New York City police officer, and I am extremely proud of him. And I love him very much.

I also loved being married to a fireman, and felt privileged to be part of that world. Of course, it wasn't easy, because being a firefighter, especially in New York City, is a very dangerous profession. And I worried about Dan a lot. For example, one day when Dan was working I decided to go shopping in Soho. As I was walking down the street, all of a sudden I could see and smell smoke, and hear sirens. My heart began palpitating a mile a minute. I was going to see Dan going into a fire! It turned out to be a minor one, but watching him and his brothers running into a smoke-filled building was very unnerving. In fact, I always felt like he was going off to war when he went to work, because we never knew what the day might bring, especially in New York City. And there were times, too, that I would wake out of a sound sleep thinking that he was in a burning building or in some other sort of danger. But it was all in a day's work for those brave men and women.

His being a fireman also meant that our schedules were vastly different—nine-to-five versus around-the-clock. Even so, we managed to work it out, particularly on holidays. Sometimes that meant having turkey at noon on Thanksgiving so Dan could be at work by the time his six o'clock tour began. I also remember once bringing cheesecake to the boys at the firehouse when Dan had to work on Easter Sunday. Not that I minded going to the firehouse. I loved going there, and often met him there after work, or stopped by to say hello on my way home. There was always so much going on, lots of jokes and laughter. It's not that the boys weren't serious about their work. It's just that most of the training and drills were done when I wasn't there, either early in the morning or later in the day. And they were certainly serious when the tones came in for a run. They would quickly jump into their gear and be off, each man in his assigned position. It was always a little nerve-wracking when a run came in while I was there. I would pray for all of them, as I always do whenever I see an emergency vehicle rushing to a scene. Our fire department, police department, EMS, and armed forces—all these brave men and women—are truly our heroes. Theirs is a noble calling.

Because of my relationship with Dan, I also always felt very safe in New York City, as though I had the entire FDNY and NYPD protecting me. For example, one day before we were married, I stopped at Ladder 5 on my way home from work to see Dan. But the boys were out on a run, and since I couldn't be sure of how long they'd be, I decided to go home. Leaving the firehouse, I turned the corner and walked down King Street towards Varick. It was a beautiful, warm summer evening. But as I was approaching Varick Street a man came toward me saying inappropriate things, and I got very nervous. As he got closer he became more aggressive, and I didn't know what to do. But then, as soon as I turned the corner onto Varick, I saw Ladder 5 coming towards me. Stopping, I turned to the man, and said, "That's my boyfriend in his fire truck." Need I say more? The guy just took off. Dan called to me, "Get in the truck," and the boys pulled me up into the back cab and took me back to the firehouse.

Most of all, though, we just loved living in New York. We often went out to dinner on Friday nights, if Dan was off. Sometimes he would meet me in midtown and we would bounce around Soho, Tribeca, and then head home to Battery Park City. Sometimes Craig would join us as well. In fact, we loved living there so much that we were actually thinking about buying an apartment there, at least we were for a while . . .

CHAPTER THREE

September 11, 2001

Yea, though I walk through the shadow of the valley of death I will fear no evil; for thou art with me; thy rod and thy staff they comfort me.
Psalms 23:2

ON THE MORNING OF SEPTEMBER 11, 2001, Dan got up early to make me breakfast. That morning it was an asparagus omelet. He is so wonderful. He wanted to make sure I had a good start to the day, and he does make the best omelets. When I got dressed, I put on my lavender Ann Taylor pants suit so I could wear a lower heel. We were expecting visitors in the office from the bank's corporate headquarters in Charlotte, North Carolina, and I knew I would be spending a good portion of my day running around.

I got to my office in the North Tower of the World Trade Center at around 7:30 to help get ready for the meetings. Once they were underway, and I got my day up-to-speed, I was contemplating if I should run downstairs to the concourse to do a few quick errands or stay in case anyone needed anything. I was still asking myself "Should

I stay or should I go?" when all of a sudden, a thunderous explosion, louder than anything I had ever heard, ripped through the building. It was 8:46:30. I was thrown out of my chair as the building swayed from side to side several times. The air was immediately filled with smoke and a terrible smell that I didn't recognize. (It was only later that I learned it was jet fuel.) Tiles were falling from the ceiling, lights were swaying, and people were trying to regain their balance. I heard one of our associates yell, "Get to the staircase!" Of course, I knew immediately that something terrible had happened. Even so, the first thing that came to me was a voice saying, "This is not your time. We are with you. Your brother is with you." And I knew he was with Dan too. To this day, I don't know exactly whose voice I heard at that moment. It may have been my angel, or a guiding spirit. It may even have been Jesus. What I do know is that it was loud and clear. And that whoever it was, he was with us, those of us who would survive, as well as those of us who were passing over.

The fire was spreading, but by the grace of God we were right near a stairwell, and were able to get into it before the flames engulfed the entire floor. The plane had gone in from the ninety-third to the ninety-ninth floors, and there was significant damage not only in the direct impact area but above and below it as well. We were on the eighty-first floor, and we didn't see anyone coming down from above us at all. (I did, though, later hear about a handful of survivors from the floors above us, including one from eighty-nine.) Standing in the stairwell, everyone managed to stay calm, but I must say it was terrifying.

My heart was palpitating a mile a minute, and I was thinking, we're up eighty-one stories. How are we getting out of here? As I turned back quickly to get my handbag,

Ben Leavitt, one of my associates, grabbed me by the hand and said, "Forget it. We're going now." Thank you, Ben. That bag would have slowed me down. But walking down eighty-one flights in heels, even low ones—I refused to take my shoes off—is no easy feat. Every second mattered. Fortunately, there were emergency lights in the stairwell so we could see. We begin making our way down, and as we did what was coming through to me was "You and Dan will be blessed with a beautiful life. You will go north." And as these thoughts came to me, I had a vision of green trees.

We made our way down to the Sky Lobby on the forty-fourth floor, but as we entered it there was another massive explosion. I didn't know it at the time, but it was the other plane crashing into the South Tower. I was afraid to look out of the window, but out of the corner of my eye I could see flames and debris flying through the sky. We waited for what seemed like a long time in the Sky Lobby, and then were directed to a different stairwell. But that one wasn't moving at all. Realizing that we couldn't stay there, Ben squeezed us into yet another stairwell, and we began our descent. It was very warm, and the lower we got the more crowded it became. Smoke began filtering into the stairwell, and as I looked around I could see that several people were drenched in sweat. Even so, we were all relatively calm. There was even some small talk. Someone said that a small charter plane had hit the building—at least that's what we thought at the time. Ben and I were worrying about his wife, who worked on the thirty-third floor of the South Tower, but usually began her day a little later than we began ours. (I found out later that she was caught in the courtyard when the first plane hit, an extremely dangerous place to be. Thankfully, she was fine.)

When we reached the twenties we began seeing firemen, which was a great relief. I knew many of them because of Dan, including Lieutenant Vincent Giammona. I grabbed his arm and said, "Vinny, be safe," and began praying for him and all the "boys" coming up the stairwell. His face looked different then I had ever seen it. He was always laughing, joking, and smiling. Not that day. I will never forget the look on his face. He never came back down that stairwell. He left behind his beautiful wife, Theresa, and four lovely daughters—Nicolette, Toni-Ann, Daniella, and Francesca—as well as a very loving, devoted family. Heartbreaking.

As we were making our way down to the lower floors I suddenly felt an incredible sense of urgency. We reached the tenth floor, the ninth floor, the eighth floor, that feeling of urgency growing every second. By the time we got to seven I was yelling at people (and I hardly ever yell), "Let's go, move it, move it, we're almost out of here." Finally, we came out of the stairwell, and found ourselves on the mezzanine level overlooking the lobby. I couldn't believe the destruction. When the Tower was hit, the building twisted, and the thick lobby glass was blown out. There was glass everywhere. I probably heard the sound of bodies dropping too, but I was in a state of shock. We walked down one of the escalators to the concourse, where all the shops were. It was like a scene from a movie—complete devastation. Store windows were blown out, there was water pouring from the ceiling, and there was smoke in the air. There was also a chain of World Trade Center Security and emergency workers screaming at us, "RUN! RUN! HURRY! RUN!" It was horrifying.

I ran with all my strength, and came out of the building near the Borders bookstore. God had been good to me. There was flaming debris all around, but I didn't get hurt. I glanced at my watch. It was 9:55. An hour and nine minutes had passed.

ON SEPTEMBER 11, 2001, DAN was no longer working on Ladder 5. One day earlier in the year, on Good Friday, Dan had gone to work, and I was cleaning up the kitchen, when I heard the front door of our apartment being unlocked. It was Dan. To my amazement, he had just walked out of Ladder 5/Engine 24 and was AWOL (Absent Without Leave), something he had never done before. He had been having trouble with another fireman at the station, someone he just referred to as "The Tool," who was always looking to start a fight with him. And that morning "The Tool" had gotten in his face again. Dan was a lot bigger and stronger than this guy and could have easily killed him. But in order to avoid an altercation, he told his immediate officer, Lieutenant Mike Warchola, that he had to leave. Although we had no way of knowing it at the time, in a strange way "The Tool" helped save my husband's life.

After doing some soul searching, Dan decided to transfer out of Ladder 5, the Ladder truck he chauffeured, and go back up to the Bronx to work in Ladder 31. He was certain of his decision, but terribly distraught as he loved being the chauffeur of Ladder 5. Soho and the Village, which were the areas he covered, were truly our playground. He was five minutes from our home. And he was giving it all up just because of this one person.

As it happens, this occurred during Holy Week, and we had just watched a movie on television about Jesus. At the end of the film, Jesus declares, "I will be with you always to the end of time." So the following week, every morning when I left for work, I would say to Dan, "Just remember, Jesus said, 'I will be with you always.'" I knew deep down in my heart that there was a powerful reason for all of this happening, and I tried to explain it to Dan. I kept saying, "We can't see the reason for this right now, but it's huge, it is so powerful. This is part of God's plan." I felt this so strongly. And I was right. It was the beginning of Jesus' plan to save my husband's life on September 11. We are certain of this.

Although he was then working at Ladder 31 in the Bronx, several days before September 11, Dan's captain asked him to go down to Engine 10/Ladder 10 for a thirty-day detail. That station, also known as Ten House, is on Liberty Street, and sat not only at the foot of the Towers but across the street from our home. Ten House frequently had manpower shortages, as it was tough for most firemen to get to it. Even so, when Dan called me with the news I immediately got the sickest feeling in my solar plexus, and had a vision of the Towers exploding. It was a vision that I'd had several times in the past, although I had never realized what its significance might be.

On the morning of September 11, though, Dan wasn't at Ten House. He was off-duty and was in a classroom in Staten Island preparing for his upcoming lieutenant's exam. He had just settled in when someone came running into the room screaming that two planes had just crashed into the World Trade Center. Running to the window, he could see the smoke streaming into the clear blue sky, but he couldn't see anything else. It was only after he ran out of the building and got into his truck that he could tell what had happened. He tried to count the stories of the North Tower to determine if I was above or below the fire, but wasn't able to. So he began calling my office. I normally picked up on the first ring, so when he got my voicemail he assumed I was already evacuating. He thought I would be going to the roof and would be evacuated from there.

Determined to get to Ten House as quickly as possible, he flew across the Verazzano Bridge into Brooklyn. On the Gowanus Expressway a police officer was stopping every car, but Dan flashed his FDNY shield out of his window and was waved on. He was doing sixty-five to seventy miles an hour as he headed toward the Brooklyn-Battery Tunnel, and got through it just as the buses were starting to get backed up. Parking his truck on West Street, directly in front of the Downtown Athletic Club, he jumped out and ran up the street. When he got to Rector Street, he saw cops covering up a torso with a yellow plastic sheet. There were body parts all over the street—he's told me that it looked like a meat locker had exploded. There was also flaming debris from the planes as well as from the Towers. He had to watch very carefully where he was running. In his twenty-plus years as a fireman he had never experienced anything like this.

ONCE I WAS OUT OF the building, I just began walking. I had gone about a block when I ran into one of our doormen, Richard Cotrich, and asked him if he knew what happened. He said we were under attack, and that two planes had hit the World Trade Center. When I turned around to look at the buildings, I could see both Towers flaming. That horrific sight is forever etched into my brain. I was continuing to walk down the block when, all of a sudden I heard this incredible rumbling sound. It was 9:58:59, and the South Tower was starting to come down. I remember looking down at the ground and thinking, "Maybe this is my time. Maybe I am going to die. By the grace of God I managed to get out of the building okay, but now it's happening all over again, a one-two punch. Maybe this is it. After walking down eighty-one flights of stairs, how am I going to outrun this thing? Which way is this building going to fall?"

A New York City police officer, who I wish I could thank personally, took me by the hand, along with another associate from my office, and led us into the subway station at Church and Dey Street. We went deeper and deeper into the station, hitting dead ends, finding water all over the place, and I began wondering if I was going to be buried alive. The sound of the Tower falling was deafening, and to this day I am very uneasy with any type of rumbling sound. Within seconds—or at least so I learned, as I had no sense of time—the rumbling ceased. A voice in my head said, "Out," meaning get out of this subway station, and "Right," meaning to turn right. Leaving the police officer and my associate, I got out of the subway and stepped into the gray snow. Outside there was nothing but dead silence. I was soaking wet, and then covered by the gray snow falling all around me. I recall asking where the Towers were, as I was very disoriented. "Are they behind me?" I asked someone, and they told me they were. I remember people were yelling at me to cover my mouth, but thinking, "What good will that do now?"

IN THE MEANTIME, DAN HAD arrived at Ten House at the same time that other guys were starting to come in. Lieutenant Sean O'Mally was putting a crew together, and Dan put on his gear and joined it, preferring to be on a team than by himself. Thinking that I was still in the North Tower, he wanted to get to me, but he knew he had a job to do. Waiting for the lieutenant to get everyone together, he was talking with Pete Bielfeld, of Ladder 42, when he realized that he needed a tool. His captain, Paul Mallory, gave it to him, and he was about to walk out of the firehouse when a firefighter stuck his arm out to block him and said, "Holy shit, here it comes." Looking up, Dan saw the top of the South Tower beginning to lean—it was no longer standing straight up. At that moment, looking into the street, Dan saw an Asian man with a briefcase handcuffed to his wrist who had been hit by a part of an airplane and was screaming for help. Dropping everything, he grabbed the man and pulled him to the back of the firehouse. He covered the man with his body as best he could, then hunkered down behind a three- or four-foot brick wall.

That's when the South Tower came crashing down around them. It was 9:58:59. The sound was deafening, like the roar of a jet engine, and there was debris falling everywhere, flying past them with such force that it was destroying everything around them. Ladder 4, which was down the block from the firehouse, was later found buried four stories down. At first, Dan says, he couldn't breathe—it felt like he was swallowing cotton—but eventually he was able to control his breathing without hyperventilating. His back and his leg were also hurting him, although he wouldn't realize for several days exactly what was wrong with them. It was a true miracle that neither he nor the

Asian man was killed. And then, as quickly as it came, it ended. Even so, Dan found himself in the middle of a thick black cloud, and couldn't see a thing. When the black cleared slightly into gray, he dragged the injured man out of the back door of the firehouse and turned him over to the EMT paramedics who were on Thames Street.

Making his way back "outside," Dan darted across the street to the Deutsche Bank building, because he was keenly aware of the dangers of falling glass from hi-rises. He knew that it can easily blow out and cause deadly damage. The entire front of the building was gone. It was then that Dan realized it was the South Tower that had come down, and thought that, since I was in the North Tower, I must still be all right. Since I had worked in that building prior to moving to the World Trade Center, he knew there was a day care center in the building's lobby, and checked it to see if everyone had been evacuated. He tended to some folks, and told them to go to the back of the lobby where they would be secure.

As he came back out of the building he saw Mel Hazel, who had befriended him when he was just a kid who wanted to be a fireman. But Mel didn't recognize him at all because he was covered in soot. "Hey, 31," Mel said, referring to the number on Dan's helmet, and Dan said, "Hey, Mel, its me, Dan." Mel said, "Danny!" and they hugged. He told Mel that I was on the eighty-first floor of the North Tower, and that he had to get to me. Although at the time Mel wasn't at all sure that I'd made it out, he never said as much to Dan. Instead, he gave Dan his cell phone so he could call our apartment to see if I was home. At that point Dan wanted to begin his search for me and Mel wanted to go to the Command Center on West Street. But as they began walking up Albany Street a cop came running toward them shouting that the North Tower was shaking and was going to come down any second. Mel began to run, but Dan grabbed him and said, "Come with me." They ran towards the Deutsche Bank building, and ducked behind a thin cement pillar under the overhang of the building.

Then there was another roar, more rocks flying through the air, more flaming debris carried by the wind. It was 10:28:22. The North Tower had fallen. Shoulder-to-shoulder they hunkered down with everything flying past them and hitting the backs of their necks, just waiting for the big hit that, by the grace of God, never came. Dan has often told me how, despite the circumstances, he felt a sense of comfort being there with Mel. As soon as the noise stopped they crawled from behind the pillar. Everything around them was dark. Dan tried turning his flashlight on, but he was shaking too much. Then, scratching at the floor with his hands, he realized they were in the street. As they crawled through the street, the darkness began to fade into light, and Dan realized how quiet it had become, as quiet as if snow were falling. Gray snow.

Dan said to Mel, "I have to find Jean," and headed toward our home in Battery Park City. As he made his way through the debris on the streets, everything around him was burning—cars, fire apparatus . . . all on fire. He saw Lieutenant Billy Ryan from Ladder 5, who was taking names of survivors, and gave him his name to add to the list. He also ran into Captain Mallory, and asked about the crew. Ten House had lost six brothers: Lieutenant Gregg Atlas, Captain (Ret.) James Corrigan, Lieutenant Stephen Harrell, firefighter Paul Pansini, firefighter Sean Tallon, and firefighter Jeffrey J. Olsen.

Even while Dan was trying to find me, I continued walking through the gray snow toward Chinatown. I was trying to find a phone that worked, asking FBI agents, the police, but no one could get a line out. A business rolled its iron gate down in my face. And all I wanted was some help, just a phone, so I could call Dan and let him know I was all right. I assumed he was still at school studying for the lieutenants' test, but I wanted to call his firehouse in the Bronx because I figured they'd be able to relay a message to him. I was desperate to get to him and my family. I kept walking until, just as I got to Chinatown, I heard another rumbling noise, this time at more of a distance. The North Tower had collapsed.

As I walked on in a complete state of shock, this lovely young man asked me if I needed something. I asked him for water and a phone. He invited me into his home, but I was too afraid, and still in shock. He did bring me a phone, though, as well as a chair to sit on, and I was able to call Dan's firehouse in the Bronx. How I ever remembered the number, as he had just transferred there, is beyond me. I told them I was OK, in case he called. My new friend, Jameson Gong, and I proceeded to the main firehouse in Chinatown. Dan had always told me that if I had a problem, I should go to the nearest firehouse. This one was Engine 9/Ladder 6, Jay Jonas' firehouse.

There were a few boys in the house watch, the small room by the door of the firehouse. I told them who I was and that I had been on the eighty-first floor of the North Tower when the plane hit. I also told them that my husband was a fireman, and that I felt I needed to do something to help. So I began answering the phones in the house watch. The calls started coming in from parents, wives, and family members, asking about their loved ones.

The boys started coming in on recall. As they walked into the house watch, they looked at me—disheveled, wet, and covered with gray dust—and, I'm sure, wondered what I was doing there. It was very unnerving to see them put on their bunker gear to head down to the World Trade Center—I was so afraid for all of them. And all the while I was still thinking my husband was in Staten Island.

As I watched the events on the TV in the house watch, I thought to myself, "My family is going to look at this and think I'm dead. I need to let them know I'm okay." We were not able to get any phone lines out, but a couple walking by the firehouse offered me their phone. I remember the woman saying to me, "This phone will work," and I was able to call my parents in Pennsylvania. My mom was crying on the phone saying, "Sweetheart, sweetheart . . . ." She and my dad had actually been out shopping that morning, and were in a parking lot when a man banged on their window and told them that two planes had hit the World Trade Center. They frantically raced home to watch the coverage on television, and couldn't believe what they were seeing. Of course, they knew that I worked in the North Tower, and were sure that I had perished. I told my mom to call my mother-in-law, June, and tell her that Dan was in Staten Island at a class. Eventually the boys in the station put me in a room in the back to try and rest. But I kept wanting to get to Dan. I wanted him to know that I was alright. I couldn't sit still, so I just paced the floor.

HOPING TO FIND ME AT home, Dan made his way toward Battery Park City. As soon as he got to our building he asked the doorman—Arturo was on that morning—if he had seen me. Arturo didn't even recognize Dan, but told him that he hadn't seen me. Climbing the nine flights to our apartment, he banged on our door, but there was no answer. And he was sure, at that moment, that I was gone. Totally overwhelmed, he leaned back against the wall, slid down to the floor, and cried.

Once he regained his composure, he went back downstairs and outside. He sat on the bench overlooking the Hudson River where he used to wait for me every night. And at that moment, a photo was taken of him. It's a photo that is in countless books about 9/11, a photo I still have difficulty looking at, because of the grief and despair on his face.

Even then, though, he wouldn't give up, and decided to try our apartment again. He had no keys on him, so he called Virgil, one of our building staff, to help him chisel through the lock. Just as they got the door open, the phone began ringing. It was my Aunt Lee asking about my whereabouts. Dan replied, "I don't know where Jean is," and Aunt Lee kept screaming, "Is she dead? Is she dead?" Dan cut her off, and said, "I don't know. I have to find her." But no sooner had he hung up than another call came in. This time it was his father asking if everyone was okay. Dan told him he was all right, but added, "I don't know where Jean is."

That's when his father said, "Oh, I know where Jean is. She's OK. Do you know where the main firehouse in Chinatown is?" "Of course I do," he said, and immediately called the firehouse and asked if they had a beautiful redhead over there? "Yes," they told him, "she's in the TV room." So he ran down nine flights of stairs and out through the courtyard to his truck on West Street. And, finally, somewhere around noon, my wonderful husband appeared, not in civilian clothes as I had expected, but in his bunker gear, covered with debris, and with blood red eyes. I was stunned to see him like that. I asked him, "Where were you?" and he responded, "You don't want to know." We just hugged each other so tightly. And all I could think was, "Thank you, Jesus, for the gift of this life."

My high school graduation photo.

My wonderful grandmother, "Nanny," and her dog, Benji.

An early photo of my dad and me at my Aunt Mary's house.

My sweet brother, John.

Dan as a Junior Fireman in Brentwood, New York.

Dan as a newly-appointed fireman at Engine 88.

Dan as a seasoned veteran at Ladder 112.

The site of the Deutsche Bank building, where Dan hunkered down with Mel Hazel during the collapse of the North Tower.

Dan and his brothers Tim Gallagher and Marty O'Neill at the end of a day's recovery work.

One of the many destroyed fire trucks and emergency vehicles in Battery Park City.

World Trade Center dust and debris in our apartment.

THIS TRUCK WAS DONATED BY BANK OF AMERICA AND ITS ASSOCIATES
TO THE FIRE DEPARTMENT OF THE CITY OF NEW YORK
IN MEMORY OF THE COURAGE AND SACRIFICE OF SO MANY
IN RESPONDING TO THE TRAGIC EVENTS OF SEPTEMBER 11, 2001,
AND OF THE LOYALTY AND COMMITMENT OF OUR ASSOCIATES
WHO LOST THEIR LIVES EVEN AS THEY TRIED TO SAVE THE LIVES OF OTHERS.

LIAM COLHOUN

SUSAN CLANCY CONLON

ROBERT (BOBBY) HUGHES

A plaque bearing the names of the three Bank of America associates who were killed on 9/11. Bank of America donated three fire trucks in their honor.

Dan and me with our new friend, Jameson Gong, who helped me in Chinatown.

Dan and me with my parents, Amy and John, at their fiftieth wedding anniversary.

Dan and me at his retirement luncheon.

A dinner in Bronxville with Dennis Smith, Jim McGlynn, Kathleen Walter, Dan, me, and Wendy and Mel Hazel.

Home sweet home in Pennsylvania.

Our precious girls, Ruby and Serafina.

My stepson, Craig, Dan, and me at the 9/11 World Trade Center Steel dedication in Hemlock Farms.

CHAPTER FOUR

After the Deluge

*Fear not . . . I will strengthen thee . . . I will
help thee.*
Isaiah 41:10

Having found each other at last, Dan and I just stood in the firehouse with our arms around each other for a long time. We were very lucky, and grateful, to be reunited, particularly so early in the day. People were ending up in New Jersey, Brooklyn, and other places, not knowing where their loved ones were. We knew we couldn't go back to our apartment, at least not yet—it was right in the middle of a war zone—but we couldn't stay in the firehouse either. Dan felt that we should go to my parents, that I needed to be with them, and that they needed to see me. We were also afraid there might be other attacks, and felt that we needed to get out of the city as fast as possible.

Leaving the firehouse, Dan and I made our way back toward West Street, where he had left his truck. Fortunately, it had survived the collapses, although, like everything in the area, it was covered with gray dust. We jumped in the truck and got on the FDR Drive going north, heading for my parents' house in northeast Pennsylvania. Although it was a beautiful, blue-sky day, there were no planes flying in the air, and it was quite eerie. We had to stop many times so Dan could rinse his eyes out. They were still blood red from the dust, fumes, and smoke at Ground Zero, and it was making it very difficult for him to see. (In fact, for the next few mornings he would have to pry them open with his fingers because the concrete dust had fused them shut while he slept.) I don't remember a great deal about that two-hour drive, but I do recall a few things. I remember telling Dan that "This is like another birthday for us. As if God has given us another birthday, a second chance at life." I also remember phoning Debbie Terlizzi, my boss' wife, and her yelling on the phone, "He's safe, he's safe!" I was so relieved. I remember, too, walking into a rest stop and feeling like everyone was staring at me. I know I was a bit of a mess, but in the days following 9/11 I always had a strange sensation that people were staring at me. It may have been because I couldn't walk properly for a few days—my legs were as stiff as boards after walking down eighty-one flights of stairs. Or maybe it was just that the angels surrounding me were shining through, and people could sense it.

When we arrived at my parents' home they were of course very relieved to see us, but also shocked to see what we looked like. It was very upsetting for them. My dad cleaned Dan's bunker gear and uniform, and my Aunt Patricia and Uncle Frank brought over some clothing that belonged to my cousin Lizzie—just sweats, a tee shirt, and sneakers. My beautiful lavender Ann Taylor pantsuit was a mess, still soaked, covered with dust, and full of shards of glass. My shoes were too. My clothing also had the horrendous 9/11 odor that would permeate the site for months. I kept washing my face, too, because it felt like there was glass in it. Even a facial a few weeks later didn't help. (I would also have a rash all over my body for months afterward.)

We stayed at my parents overnight. Over and over again my dad kept saying, "You both dodged the bullet." Sitting in my parents' living room, we watched the events unfold on TV, and it was nothing less than surreal. I also started making phone calls. The first was to my dearest friend, Debbie, who had phoned my mother earlier in the day looking for us. Debbie and I met when we were just ten years old and have been lifelong friends. I called to let her know we were both okay. The second was to my "Earth Angel," Lucy. Lucy is one of my dearest friends, and I've known her for more than twenty years. She is a smart, lovely, sweet, gentle, caring person who helps all those she encounters. We discuss everything under the sun, from family issues, to politics, to real estate. I trust her and value her judgment implicitly. She knew I worked downtown, but didn't realize exactly where I worked. As it happens, her son-in-law is also a survivor. He worked for a small firm in the South Tower and, fortunately for him, they were told to leave as soon as the North Tower was hit.

After I spoke to Lucy I began making phone calls about our credit cards, licenses, bank cards, etc. Remember, I'd left my bag on the eighty-first floor when my associate, Ben Leavitt, told me we had to get out, and we needed to establish our credentials because we knew we wouldn't be able to get home for a while. Our lives had become scrambled eggs in a pan. Although we didn't quite realize it at the time, on that fateful day everything we knew had changed—our careers, our workplaces, our home, and everything around them. Nothing would ever be the same again, although we couldn't see that at the time. We are still trying to understand everything we lost that day.

The following day, September 12, we headed back to Manhattan. Dan had to get back to begin search and rescue immediately, even though he was really hurting physically. My parents wanted me to stay in Pennsylvania, but I refused. The thought of Dan going back to the city without me was terrifying. We needed to be together. But it was a difficult trip, mostly because we were heading home and apprehensive about what we were going to encounter. Crossing the George Washington Bridge, we got onto the FDR Drive and began to make our way down to lower Manhattan. Many of the streets were closed, but when Dan held up his shield and identified himself, we were able to get through. As we got closer to Ground Zero, I just knew we were going to see my stepson, Craig, and just as we got near Battery Park City, there he was. The military was there in force, and he had been deployed with the National Guard. Although Dan had already called to tell him we were all right, we all needed to see each other, and we hugged and kissed, so grateful for that gift.

It was twilight when we arrived in Battery Park City, and it was a typical, slightly warm, end-of-summer evening. We couldn't park the truck near our apartment building, so we left it a few blocks away and walked. The first thing we noticed was that all of our streets were covered with huge beams from the Towers. It was like a graveyard of steel. And as we walked, we realized we were walking in several inches of debris. It was ankle- to knee-deep, and it was horrifying—concrete, dust, papers, shoes, baby carriages, water bottles . . . another memory etched into my brain. And our beautiful building was blacked out. Our superintendent, Kenny, was sitting at the main entrance like a sentinel. He told us he was glad to see us. A lot of people would say, "It's so good to see you" in the days that followed, as they weren't sure about either of us. And we would reply, "It's good to be seen."

We walked up the nine floors to our apartment with a flashlight. We were thinking that we would be able to sleep there, but that proved impossible. Dan had broken the dead bolt on the front door the day before in his effort to find me, so we couldn't lock the door securely. Also, September 11 was a beautiful, picture perfect day, without a cloud in the sky, and I had left the windows open when I went to work. But now it was very warm in the apartment—it felt like there was no air. And our home was covered with debris, the dust of pulverized furniture, glass, concrete, equipment, and souls, many, many souls. It was very strange being in the apartment again. We loved living there so much. Our windows had faced the Towers, and it was the most soothing, beautiful sight, especially in the evening. Every day when I walked down the block on my way home from work I would say to myself, "I can't believe I live here." Now we were wondering what we would do, and where we were going to live. We grabbed some clothing and tried to secure the apartment. I was looking in the phone book for a hotel room. But the phones weren't working so we just decided to head towards midtown, away from this war zone.

We began walking towards the site where the Towers had stood. But I could feel the soul energy of the three thousand people who had just been killed, and I couldn't go any further. It was as if my angels were holding me back and trying to protect and comfort me. It was unbelievably heartbreaking, heart-wrenching, and still so incredibly frightening. The devastation was simply incomprehensible. I will never forget what it felt like, and what I had witnessed.

We made our way uptown, and ended up at a Best Western Hotel near the Empire State Building. There was a firehouse directly across the street, Engine 1/Ladder 24, and we parked our truck there. It was there that we saw the first list of "Members Missing." Dan's dear friend, Andy Desperito, who he worked with in Bushwick, was on the list, but in the next several days we would learn of many others. One of them was Vinny Giammona, Dan's lieutenant at Ladder 5. Dan had been the chauffeur at Ladder 5 and drove Vinny often. They had the best time working together. Vinny was always all fired up—he loved his double espressos. He also loved to tease me at firehouse events, like Christmas parties and picnics. He would always say, "Nice of you to stop by to see how the other half lives." And I loved being with those men and their families, all their beautiful children running around and having a ball. I may well have been the last one to see Vinny alive. It was he I had seen coming up the stairwell of the North Tower as I was coming down. I will never forget the look on his face—it is forever etched into my memory. Vinny Giammona leaves behind a beautiful wife, four daughters who worshipped the ground he walked on, and a loving family. To this day I think of him often. They are all in my prayers.

Another one of the brothers we lost was Mike Warchola, Dan's other lieutenant. Dan loved to torture Mike, constantly giving him the business about his exercising on a treadmill while smoking a cigarette with the filter torn off. When they would jump on the truck for a run, Dan would say, "Lieu, you know where this address is?" And Mike would scream at him, "You're the chauffeur, don't you know?" But even though Dan loved to torture him, they were best buddies. Mike was about to retire and was doing his last tour of duty on the morning of 9/11. His body was one of the first to be recovered. We know he suffered. Mike leaves behind two lovely children and a loving family. May you rest in peace, Mike. We miss you.

WE CHECKED INTO THE BEST Western, and had just taken showers and settled into our room when we heard alarms going off and were told to evacuate. Another evacuation. My heart palpitating, I started to grab my jewelry, but Dan yelled at me that we had to leave NOW. We left everything in the hotel room. We were told there was a bomb scare in the Empire State Building, which was just a few feet away from the hotel. It was all too much. We had to get away, so we just jumped into the truck. I was shaking, my legs were weak, and I was still disoriented. We proceeded north, looking for somewhere else we could stay. The only place I could think of was the Helmsley Park Lane. We parked the truck in the hotel's parking garage, and limped into the hotel with no bags, no money, and no credit cards. In fact, we had nothing with us except what we were wearing. We told them who we were and where we'd been. They gave us robes and checked us in. My only request at the front desk was, "A low floor, please."

Two or three days later, after Dan left the hotel to continue searching at Ground Zero, I knew I couldn't just sit in the room. So I went across the street to Bank of America's offices at 9 West 57th Street, to see my boss, Lou Terlizzi. It was great to see LT again. He and some of his staff were very surprised to see me. They knew I was all right, as I had spoken to LT's wife a few days earlier, but they also knew we lived in Battery Park City and, under the circumstances, didn't expect to see me so soon. Of course, I knew that LT had made it too, but I didn't know how. He told me the story.

He had been in a conference room on the other side of the floor from me. When he heard the explosion, he told me, "My first reaction was we had been hit by a plane . . . I thought a small plane. The lights fell down and the ceiling tiles did as well. I know the floor was tilted, because I remember running downhill to my office to get my phone. You could also smell the aviation fuel as it started to come through the ceiling. I remember yelling for everyone to get to the stairwells, but a few people went back to their desks and sat down. It was shock, I think. I grabbed them and pushed them towards the stairwell. I did one last run around the floor, and as soon as I saw no one was left, I headed for the stairwell myself. The descent was very slow and when we got to the Sky Lobby on the forty-fourth floor it was a madhouse. A thousand or so people trying to get into the same stairwell. I went around to the other side, found an open stairwell, and went back to get whoever I could find. Then we went down that stairwell.

"It was somewhere between the thirtieth and thirty-fifth floors where we meet the firefighters coming up the stairs with all their gear. They were exhausted. I grabbed some gear and carried it back up a couple of floors and passed it off to another guy like me, and told him to carry it up two floors and pass it on. When we hit the tenth floor, we finally encountered the sprinklers—they hadn't gone off above ten—so the last ten floors were like a rainforest. We finally came out in the concourse behind a store that was being renovated. All the glass from the stores on the concourse had blown out due to the compression of the building. I sloshed my way to the Church Street exit, came out, and looked back at the building. That's when I saw how bad it was. People jumping and all the smoke and fire. I was out for about fifteen seconds, walking backwards looking up, and had just walked onto Church Street when the South Tower came down right in front of my eyes. I started to run towards Fulton Street but was quickly covered by the cloud. I found a stairwell to hide in, and I was still in the stairwell when the North Tower came down. Once I could see at all, I took off and just kept heading north towards that clear blue sky."

Talking with LT that day in the Bank of America's offices, he reminded me of something I had said to him just a few days before 9/11. We had been discussing efforts he was making to help out a friend. He told me he was feeling underappreciated, and was very upset about it. I told him that he was a good person, someone who always took care of his family and his friends, and that the good things he does will come back to him in a positive way. And that day, when he brought it up, he said, "Jean, you were right. It does come back. We all made it out." Then he hugged me. Unfortunately, though, there were actually three of us who didn't make it out—Susan Clancy Conlon, Liam Joseph Colhoun, and Robert T. (Bobby) Hughes. Susan was a very loving mother to Kimberly and devoted wife to John. Liam's wife, Helen, and his daughter, Brigid, were the main priorities of his life. Bobby adored his parents and loved his three beautiful sisters. May their splendid souls rest in peace.

Seeing LT that day reminded me of something else that had happened just a few days before 9/11—I saw a rainbow outside of LT's office. I was amazed, because you practically never see a rainbow in Manhattan. And it made me think of what God said to Noah after the Flood: "And the bow shall be in the cloud; and I will look upon it, that I may remember the everlasting covenant between God and every living creature of all flesh that is upon the earth." (Genesis 9:16-17) I felt sure at the time that seeing that rainbow meant something, although I didn't know what it was. Now I think I understand—it was a reminder of God's covenant with us, a reminder of his promise to never again try to destroy us.

THE WEEKEND FOLLOWING 9/11 DAN and I limped out of the hotel for dinner, and the hotel's owner, Leona Helmsley, was in the lobby. She asked her staff about us, and we were introduced. She couldn't have been kinder. In fact, although we had insurance to cover our stay, she told us it would be on her. We were not to worry about anything. She and her entire staff were extremely kind to us during our stay. (She subsequently presented a check for five million dollars to the New York Police and Fire Widows' and Children's Benefit Fund.) And for almost three weeks the Park Lane was our home. Every morning we would order a quick breakfast, then I would go to the office and Dan would go to Ground Zero for search and rescue. In the evening we would order dinner and collapse into bed.

There was also, though, what seemed like an endless series of funerals, most of which Dan attended and some of which I did. So many had been lost. One of them, we learned, was Brian Hickey, the Captain of Rescue 4. I had heard a lot from Dan about Brian and his wife, Donna, and had just met them during the summer of 2001. They came to our apartment and we had dinner with them at one of our favorite restaurants on the Hudson, Steamer's Landing. Brian had recently returned to work after being injured in the infamous Father's Day fire, where three firefighters were killed. I was surprised that Brian was even near the World Trade Center, because Rescue 4 was housed in Queens. But on 9/11 Brian was detailed to Rescue 3 in the Bronx. Only his charred fire helmet was found. The Bethpage, New York, post office now bears his name. He left behind his loving wife, three beautiful children, and a very devoted family.

Another loss was Father Mychal Judge, the FDNY chaplain. I had the privilege of meeting Father Judge several times at memorial services and other FDNY functions. He often spoke about how fragile life is. He was well known for ministering to the homeless, people with AIDS, and alcoholics—wherever there was a need for his deep spirituality and caring prayers. On hearing that the Towers had been hit by hijacked aircraft, Father Judge rushed to the scene. He began administering last rites to victims lying on the street, and then went into the lobby of the North Tower. Shortly afterward, when the South Tower collapsed, he became one of the FDNY's first casualties. Yes, Jesus must have needed him to help the brothers and sisters, and all the other emergency workers and civilians, who were coming home. May he rest in peace.

THE WEEKS IMMEDIATELY AFTER 9/11 were a very strange time for us. The city was so silent, eerie. It seemed like the only sounds were those of sirens—police vehicles, fire trucks, ambulances, and other emergency vehicles. I would sometimes hear a baby crying on our floor. A reminder of "life," it was comforting. It was also then that we learned how badly Dan had been injured in the collapse of the South Tower. Although he was in a great deal of pain, he was running on adrenaline for several days, and forged ahead doing search and rescue. But on the morning of September 16 he couldn't get out of bed, and he went to the FDNY medical office. After a series of tests we learned that he had three herniated discs and severe nerve damage in his left leg. (The following month he was sent to the Hospital for Special Surgery, where a doctor told him his leg was beginning to atrophy and recommended surgery. Dan opted not to do it.)

One of the things that helped me, at least some, was going back to work. Bank of America's contingency site was in Secaucus, New Jersey, and LT and the remaining four hundred or so of our associates were transferred there. But because I was virtually homeless, he arranged for me to work in the Fifty-Seventh Street offices. That was particularly helpful, because the offices were right across the street from the Park Lane. I started working there on Monday, September 18, but I was very stressed and my brain wasn't functioning the way it normally does. I also found it very difficult to settle down enough to concentrate. One of the people who helped me do that was a lovely young woman named Jasmin Wilson. Her boss and their group welcomed me to their world while I was plugged into LT's world in New Jersey. Jasmin was just wonderful. She had a kind, gentle, demeanor, and it was such a pleasure working alongside her. I know I was a basket case for a while, but she will never know how much she helped me get through those first few weeks. Just being able to maintain some sort of normalcy was a godsend. She was extremely efficient and had a wonderful rapport with her boss, who was also extremely kind to me. All their little kindnesses were of tremendous value to me, especially in the beginning. I needed desperately to reshape my world back into something "normal," and this fine group of people helped me tremendously. Thank you from the bottom of my heart!

On Saturday, September 22, we made another trip downtown. I wanted to bring flowers to the site and say some prayers, but we also wanted to go to our apartment to get some clothing. We went to the apartment first, and when we got off the elevator there was the stench of rotting garbage. Our meticulously clean, wonderful building was a mess. We retrieved some personal articles, cleaned out the refrigerator, and walked over to Ground Zero. The entire landscape was so foreign. It's impossible to describe the enormity of the pile. The twisted steel, the wires, the concrete. I stood before it, shaking, praying, my legs like Jell-O. I couldn't figure out what I was looking at, or where I was standing. Everything was completely destroyed—those precious souls, our beautiful home, our beautiful Towers. It all left me speechless. When we went back to the hotel I lay down on the bed and wasn't able to talk for hours. I remember looking up at the ceiling and seeing daylight filtering in. It was in the shape of a cross.

For weeks afterward, every morning when I opened my eyes, I could almost feel the Towers coming down around me. And there were horrible dreams: Dan disappearing into a burning building, a sharpshooter in a black mask being pulled up to the hotel window and about to kill me, being in my childhood home in Brooklyn with the Taliban surrounding the house. There was also a recurring dream of trying to get home to Dan and not being able to—snow, ice, black skies, thunderstorms, rain, having to wait on a tremendous line for a bus. I still have that dream to this day, as well as an occasional "attack" dream.

Because of a *New York Post* article about us that had appeared on September 19—"Tearful Reunion—WTC Worker and Fireman Hubby Survive Disaster," with pictures of Dan and me taken in the lobby of the Park Lane—many television news shows invited us on to tell our story. But I was not in a good frame of mind to speak. More important, having survived, Dan and I knew we were truly blessed, and I didn't want to offend anyone in any way. There were so many people hurting, their losses insurmountable. What could we say?

CHAPTER FIVE

Battery Park to Bronxville

Behold, I make all things new.
Revelation 21:5

The Park Lane Hotel was lovely, but we knew that eventually we would have to go home. We made arrangements for a commercial cleaning crew to remove the debris from our apartment. It took five people several days to do it. Even so, as soon as we walked in the door I sat down and cried—I knew I could no longer live there. What was once our beautiful home was now right in the bull's-eye of Ground Zero, a war zone, a place where three thousand innocent souls had been murdered. Those souls were in our home, and I prayed for them continuously.

Then, too, there was that 9/11 odor. It was an odor unlike anything I have ever experienced, intensely strong, and foul-smelling. A combination of concrete dust, glass, smoldering fires, furniture, office equipment, and mountains of steel. That smell would stop us in our tracks. Acrid. One time Dan and I even smelled it in midtown. We just looked at each other and felt sick. After a while it seemed to go away, but then one day we came home and it was back, as if the wind had shifted. I walked into our bedroom and just lay on the bed and cried. I was frozen in space. It was so difficult living there. The smells. The noise. I never slept. We could hear equipment twenty-four hours a day. Searching for bodies all day, all night. Removing debris. Worse than their going continuously was when they stopped. You knew then that they had found something, or some one.

It seemed like every time we left our apartment we were surrounded by flatbed trucks carrying metal beams. It was awful. We looked at the mangled steel, the gaping holes in the earth, the smoldering fires. It was a sight you can't really imagine—you have to have seen it. Complete and utter devastation—like being in a living hell. The magnitude of the destruction was incomprehensible. When I look back on it now, I really don't know how we made it through. I did know, though, that we couldn't possibly begin the healing process as long as we had to keep looking at this and re-living it day after day.

Another thing I found very disturbing was that a lot of people were leaving Battery Park City, although I understood entirely why they did. But because of that, apartment prices had dropped, and people began buying apartments at the lower prices and moving in. Could you imagine how anyone could capitalize on this tragedy? One of them moved in next door to us. As I heard him hammering nails to hang pictures on the wall, he was laughing and joking. I knocked on his door to remind him to pray for the three thousand innocent souls who were in his apartment. As I left I heard him say something like "What was that all about?" He probably thought I was crazy. But I was so unbelievably stressed and upset that it was hard for me to tolerate things like this.

By the Grace of God

There were other things going on as well. The phones didn't work. There was no mail delivery, because our local post office had been closed, and we had to go to the main post office in midtown to retrieve our mail. Then there was the anthrax scare, and I was opening our mail with rubber gloves. It's not that that would have helped, I just didn't want to touch anything. It was truly a war zone—hard to get in, hard to get out. The military had set up tents on the grassy areas where we used to relax and read on the weekends. The promenade on the waterfront was fenced off. We knew we were truly blessed to have survived, but to have to see it, smell it, and live in it was very tough. We never stopped praying for the victims and their families.

One good thing that happened, after our phones began working again, was I received calls from three of my former bosses. The first one was from Arni Amster, the private investor whose financial information I had helped manage. It was so great to hear his voice. He had called the FDNY to try and find out about Dan, but they were very reluctant to give him any information as he wasn't family, although in a way he was. After some negotiating, he had been told that there were two lists of casualties and Dan Potter wasn't on either one. Another call was from Joe Gargan, the wonderful gentleman I had worked for at Elizabeth Arden many years earlier. He came from a family of firefighters, and wanted to make sure we were okay. The third call was from one of my favorite bosses, Bill Frank, who was the chief financial officer at Revlon. He called several days after he had attended a memorial service for a friend of his who was killed in the South Tower. It was so good hearing from him. He told me all about his friend. We also discussed his daughter's upcoming marriage in October. These gentlemen were all calling to check on my husband, and because they knew we lived in Battery Park City. But they all were astounded to hear exactly where I was that day—none of them had any idea that I worked at the World Trade Center.

ALTHOUGH WE MOVED BACK INTO our apartment on September 26, 2001, because we knew we couldn't live there anymore, on Saturday, October 6 we actively began looking for a new place. That day we drove up to Westchester County, just north of the city, and looked at apartments in Bronxville and Tuckahoe, New York. Again, Jesus and his angels were with us every step of the way. On October 7 we found our new home, a beautiful coop apartment in a building called Alden Place, right in the heart of Bronxville Village. The following Saturday, October 13, we attended a memorial mass for retired FDNY Captain James Corrigan, who was the fire safety coordinator in the South Tower. After the mass, we drove back to see Alden Place again, and decided it would be our home. A beautiful apartment in a beautiful town, where we could catch our breath and begin the healing process. In between going to work and attending funeral masses, we made our plans to move on December 17, 2001.

In the meantime, though, we continued living in Battery Park City, and did the best we could to keep it together. Thanksgiving that year was a particularly tough one. I had to work that Friday so we couldn't drive to Pennsylvania to see my parents. Dan's parents wanted to come to New York to spend the holiday with us. I knew they were very concerned and wanted to spend time with us, but the idea of having a holiday dinner in a war zone was very unnerving. Even so, I didn't feel I could say no to them. I don't know where I got the strength to prepare a holiday meal while we were getting ready to move to Bronxville. I know I made a traditional Thanksgiving dinner, but I don't remember what I cooked or how I shopped for it. The only thing I remember about that day is that my in-laws kept saying how nervous we were. Every little noise made us jump and ask, "What's that?" The things you do for love!

We actually closed on our apartment on our second wedding anniversary, December 12, 2001. The song, "Optimistic Voices" from "The Wizard of Oz" kept playing in my head. "You're out of the woods / You're out of the dark / You're out of the night / Step into the sun / Step into the light." In fact, Bronxville seemed like Oz to me. It was a beautiful place, with magnificent mansions in the hills and charming coops, condos, and townhouses in the heart of the village. And everything was right at your fingertips—lovely boutiques, supermarkets, fabulous restaurants, and every service you could imagine. It was like a little bit of Americana, and we were looking forward to living there.

It was six o'clock in the morning of December 17 when our bell rang and we found our movers at the front door (R-Way Moving and Storage—the best movers in the whole wide world). We were still throwing items in boxes. We were very happy to be leaving, but I had lived there for nine years, and I cried saying goodbye to our wonderful doormen. God did, though, bring us to a beautiful place. The people of Bronxville welcomed us with open arms, for which we were grateful. Perhaps most important, we went from the sound of machinery twenty-four/seven to the sound of church bells, as our home was directly across the street from a church.

Because I'm an extremely organized person, I had everything unpacked within a few days after we arrived. Dan had painted the apartment prior to our move, which helped tremendously. I was even able to put up a small tree two or three days before Christmas. We were trying to settle into our beautiful new home, but it was very difficult, because our nerves were still so raw and frayed.

One thing that helped was the Reformed Church of Bronxville's outdoor Village Pageant. They set it up every year, and it was like having the Radio City Music Hall Christmas Spectacular right outside our window. Before the start of the pageant, which portrays Jesus' birth and the arrival of the wise men, the church played choral music over loudspeakers, and we watched as folks walked from their beautiful homes into the village to share in this wondrous event. It was like a scene from Currier and Ives. It was so heartwarming, and by the end of the pageant, with snow falling gently, everyone was moved to tears. For us, that Christmas was filled with sorrow and mourning over the loss of so many, but it was also when we began to heal. I have a photo of Dan holding a Rudolph statue I had given him. He is smiling, but there is such despair on his face, in his soul. I wonder sometimes how we made it back from the edge of darkness. But of course I know, it was Jesus who pulled us through. Only He could have saved us.

ONCE WE MOVED TO BRONXVILLE, I began commuting again. I hadn't commuted to work in nine years, as I had lived in the city. Now, though, I would be on the 7:01 train to Grand Central every morning, then jump into a taxi to get to Thirty-Third Street and Sixth Avenue, where our new Bank of America offices were. I wasn't thrilled with taking the subway so, often, if I couldn't get a cab, I would walk from Grand Central to the office. But even though it was a short ride to the city, the commute was wearing me down. Everything was taking its toll on me. I was even feeling stressed every morning when the train entered the tunnel to get into Grand Central . . . still a lot of Post Traumatic Stress Disorder. And when I commuted home in the evening I always gave a sigh of relief once the train got out of that tunnel. "Another non-eventful day in New York City," I'd think, "and I am going home to my husband. Praise the Lord." My days of working in New York City were winding down. I knew I couldn't take much more of it.

One of the things that made life a little easier for us during that time was adopting a black-and-white cat. Anatole France once wrote, "Until one has loved an animal, a part of one's soul remains un-awakened," and it is certainly true. Dan had wanted to rescue a cat from a shelter, and on May 11, 2002, we found our Mitsy at the Elmsford Animal Shelter. The sign on her cage said she was fourteen- to sixteen-years-old. She had been with one family for over fourteen years when they gave her up for adoption. When I looked into her eyes they locked into mine, and as I walked around her cage her eyes followed me. And when Dan took her out of the cage, she completely relaxed in his arms as if to say, "What took you so long to get here?"

That night we took her to bed with us, and she kept throwing herself at us as though she was trying to say, "Thank you, thank you." And from then on we all slept together. We don't really know why her family gave her up, but we believe it was so this sweet, wonderful soul could be with us. She was a wonderful comfort to us, particularly on the rough days. One day when I was very upset and started to cry, she jumped up into my lap and put her paw on my heart. She truly helped us heal from the horrors we had experienced. She was so amazing—I'm convinced cats are really angels in disguise. We all lived very happily together in Bronxville.

But as much as Mitsy helped, things were still very difficult for both of us. Like me, Dan continued to travel into the city everyday, in his case to help with the recovery work at Ground Zero. But the mental and physical trauma was taking a toll on him as well, and in May 2002 he was told that, due to his injuries, he had to retire. At that point he had been with the FDNY for almost twenty years, but he'd had no intention of retiring, and he was devastated. He would have probably done twenty-five to thirty years. It would take him a long time to adjust, but I am so very grateful that he did retire, and now he is too. A few months later, in August, the commute to the city finally became too much for me, and I resigned from Bank of America. That was so difficult. I loved my job and I loved working for Lou, but everything changed on 9/11. When LT told his staff that "Jean has just resigned," everyone said, "Jean who?" They all knew that I loved working there, and couldn't imagine that I would ever quit. But I just couldn't handle the stress anymore, and I wanted to be closer to home.

Life in Bronxville was a lot different than it had been in New York City, and we were able to begin our healing process. Dan's new nickname for us was "the collapse couple"—his great sense of humor was beginning to return. Trying to recreate my job in Manhattan, I worked for a while at a small packaging company in Tuckahoe, but it was very difficult. I then decided to try something entirely different, so I went to work as the front office administrator at the Siwanoy Country Club. I also got a realtor's license, which enabled me to work in real estate on a part-time basis. Within our first year at Alden Place Dan was asked if he would run for president of the coop board. He ran, and won the position. My husband always makes tremendous improvements in his environment, leaving everything better than he found it, and this was no exception. He took wonderful control of the board and hired the appropriate individuals to keep our home (and everyone else's) running smoothly. And even though that was a full-time job for him, Dan also did 11th hour hospice work in Bronxville. I know he was a tremendous comfort to those who were passing, as well as being a source of strength for their loved ones. Yes, he continued doing God's work.

The following summer, Mel Hazel, Dan's old mentor, and his lovely wife, Wendy, invited some of us to their home for a barbecue. It was good to be together again and to meet some of their friends. While we were there, Mel prayed for all of the fallen brothers and their families, and it was so moving. The next day I had a dream—or, I should say, a visitation—from Vinny Giammona, the FDNY lieutenant I had met in the stairwell on my way out of the World Trade Center. In the dream I seemed to be at the Last Supper, but the table was Vinny's coffin, and his head had a blood-soaked bandage around it. He kept saying that he wanted me to tell his family "not to be so sad." He was showing me family photos and letters from his girls on pink stationery that said "T H O Y" across the top (although I'm not sure what those initials meant). The girls had written on the stationery, "Dad is up to no good," because their father was the ultimate prankster. When I asked him if he was alive or it was his spirit I was talking to, he said, "What do you think?" at which point I woke up shaking. When I told Dan about the dream, he told me that Vinny used to keep family photos in the firehouse and work on family photo albums in his spare time. I wasn't entirely sure what the dream meant, but I knew I had to reach out again to Vinny's wife, Theresa, and to their girls, Francesca, Toni-Ann, Nicolette, and Daniella. I sent Theresa a Kirks Folly heart locket bracelet with a note telling her about my dream, and sent the girls treats on holidays for many, many years.

In December 2004 Dan ran for fire commissioner of Eastchester. He didn't win, but he came very close to winning. Interestingly, though, the day of the election we both began wondering if this was really where we wanted to be in five years. We hadn't been thinking about it, but we began to. And then, one day in February 2005, I came home from work and Dan said to me, "Why are we living here?" My response was, "I don't know. Why *are* we living here?" So we talked for awhile about different places we might like to live, and then thought about Hemlock Farms, where my parents live in Pennsylvania. It's only an hour-and-a-half from New York City, at the place where New York, New Jersey, and Pennsylvania meet, and we knew it was a beautiful place. I got on line and found a beautiful new house, and called a realtor, Rebecca Smith of Century 21 Smith Realty Group, who made our move to Pennsylvania very easy. In the meantime, I put our coop on the market, and within three days we had an all cash offer at our asking price. So began another part of God's plan.

CHAPTER SIX

Home in Pennsylvania

*Thou has cast men to ride over our heads,
we went through fire and through water, but
thou broughtest us out into a wealthy place.*
Psalms 66:12

ON SEPTEMBER 11, 2001, AS I was making my way down from the eighty-first floor of the North Tower, I heard a voice saying, "You and Dan will be blessed with a beautiful life. You will go north." And as these thoughts came to me, I had a vision of green trees. But never in my wildest imagination could I have envisioned the beautiful life that we have been blessed with. We now live in a lovely new home in Hemlock Farms, the same community where my parents live. It really is wonderful to be just five minutes down the road from them—there is nothing as important as family. I am also very grateful that Dan had to retire at a young age, and that we both no longer have to work at the killer pace that we did for so many years in Manhattan.

Perhaps most important, it is breathtakingly beautiful here. I've never seen such beautiful skies in my life, especially the sunsets. This place has helped us heal. It's peaceful, quiet, and only an hour-and-a-half to the George Washington Bridge and New York City, if we need to go there for any reason. Everything is easier here—shopping, movies, the theater, the only tradeoff being that you need to drive a distance. The other thing I absolutely love about living here is being so close to nature and our beautiful animals. We have deer that bring us their fawns every spring (I have names for each and every one), bears, woodchucks, turkeys, squirrels, chipmunks, and a variety of birds, including blue jays, woodpeckers, and robins. I even saw a bobcat in our yard one day. They are all so magnificent. Every time one comes on to our property I say, "Thank you, Jesus, for this gift." In fact, we have been so blessed that every morning as soon as I wake up I say, "Thank you, Jesus, for the gift of this beautiful day and this beautiful life." I say it several times during the course of the day as well, and it's always the last thing I say after I've said my prayers at night and before I go to sleep. We know that we are very blessed, but we also continue to pray for those who are not as fortunate and are still suffering.

The one small setback we experienced soon after moving to Pennsylvania was that our Mitsy left us, on July 30. I knew the end was near when I left the house that morning for my exercise class, and I cried as I was trying to work out. When I came home I found that she had collapsed in her litter box. Losing her was very difficult for us, and we were in another downward spiral for a while. She now rests comfortably in the front of our home where the sun always shines.

As HAPPY AS WE ARE, though, living here has taken some adjustment. In some respects, I'm still adjusting. The biggest difficulty for me was not working, because I worked my whole life, and have found it difficult to get used to not having somewhere to go every morning. It's been a little less difficult for Dan, partly because he has to some extent been able to continue doing what he did when we lived in Manhattan. At least he's been able to do it on an administrative level—due to his injury he can no longer fight fires or do anything that requires strenuous physical activity. Practically as soon as we moved in he volunteered to do administrative work, train the firefighters, and be assistant chief of the volunteer fire company here in Hemlock Farms. He's still training our volunteer firefighters, and has developed fire safety courses for our senior community. He also volunteers as the disaster services manager for the American Red Cross for Pike and Wayne counties, and helped facilitate the opening of Red Cross shelters for our neighbors in the event of an emergency. He has also created a team of volunteers who can shelter pets on behalf of their owners in the event of an emergency.

In addition, he has just volunteered to be training coordinator of the Pike County Training Complex, which is currently being built, and will train all fire, EMS and first responders. In the meantime, he has begun scheduling classes which will be held at local schools until the facility is ready. And on top of all this, he writes informative articles and bulletins for the public, firemen, and his Red Cross associates. So my wonderful husband continues to do God's work. Just as when he was a fireman in New York City, he's still responding to dire situations like fire and natural disaster, and taking care of those in need. He is truly a wonderful human being.

Even though I don't have to get up and go to work everyday, I am still very busy as well. I do fundraising for the American Red Cross, have become a Reiki practitioner, and spend a good deal of time working with sick or wounded animals. Like a lot of our neighbors, I also volunteer at the Pike County Correctional Facility. I work as a counselor to inmates, most of whose crimes are due to drug and alcohol abuse—petty larceny, domestic issues, and others. I first got involved in the program because Dan was familiar with the facility, and encouraged me to meet with Irene Doolittle, who was director of programs at the time. Now I'm kind of an old hand at it, but I remember that, in the beginning, it was a little difficult.

The first time I went to the jail to meet her, I felt totally out of my element, and more than a little nervous. In the reception area I was told to put all my belongings in a locker—including my jewelry, except my wedding band. I then had to log in at the front desk, go through a metal detector, and show my driver's license as identification. Then I was given a visitor's number badge to wear. Since 9/11 I've had certain issues about being near exits. I always need to know I can get out quickly. Well, in jail you can't. And as I went through the first of many automatic doors that opened and then electronically "slammed" closed behind me, it was pretty unnerving. But the interview went very well, and I left thinking this would be something I would love to do. As it turned out, I was right.

My program is called "Counseling with Jean Potter," and I go in once a week and, basically, listen to the inmates and offer whatever guidance and help I can. At this point, I'm only working with women—I'm not ready for the men yet. I start each session by greeting them with a big smile and asking how they're feeling. I then talk to them about my husband and me being 9/11 survivors, and explain that just as Jesus gave us another chance at life, incarceration is giving them another chance. I tell them that it's a time of reflection, redemption, regrouping, learning new skills, and trying to manage their addictions. When I say that to them, it's always as if a light had been turned on for them, and they are wonderfully appreciative. Working with them is an extraordinary experience for me, because they are all very different from the people in the world I came from. But each one of them is a beautiful soul. Dan refers to this as "cutting edge" work, and I'm very proud of it. I am also very grateful for the opportunity, and hope that I am making a difference at least in some small way.

DAN KNEW, OF COURSE, THAT I was very upset when our Mitsy left us. I have a lot of difficulty with loss, even though I know when our loved ones leave us they are at home with Jesus where they belong, where everything is perfect, and where there is no more pain and suffering. So he decided to look for another cat for me. He found my precious Ruby in a shelter called Peaceable Kingdom, in Allentown, Pennsylvania. It was only a few weeks after Mitsy had passed, and I thought I wasn't ready, but God knew Ruby was just what I needed. "She came to mend Mama's broken heart," as I sing to her every morning, and she did so magnificently. Ruby is a gorgeous buff-and-white domestic short hair with beautiful green eyes. She is the sweetest, most loveable girl in the whole wide world, and she—along with Jesus, of course—restored my heartbroken soul.

About a year-and-a-half later, on one cold September morning, I was on my way to exercise class when I happened to look down and saw a little, black, green-eyed, shivering, flea-bitten kitten looking up at me. She was huddled in the sun trying to keep warm, and she wouldn't let anyone get close to her, except me. And she kept meowing at me, as if she was asking for my help. I immediately phoned Dan, who rushed over. When he picked her up, she curled up in his arms, and we took her home. At first I thought we would bring her to a no-kill shelter. After all, we already had Ruby, and I didn't think Ruby would want to have another cat around the house. And I did make some phone calls. "How can we keep her?" I thought. And then, "How can we give her away?" I was very distraught, and really didn't know what to do. Finally, though, we decided to bring her to a shelter.

But on our way there I said to Dan, "Let's see if Dr. Morgan [our vet] is in." Low and behold, wonderful Dr. Morgan was in, and took us immediately. We discovered that Serafina, as I had decided to call her, was approximately seven-weeks-old. We also discovered she had fleas, parasites, and a huge chunk of fur missing from behind her ear. In other words, she wasn't in good shape at all. We told Dr. Morgan we weren't sure what to do with her, and she said that if we decided to keep her, we should bring her back for a Feline Leukemia/FIV virus test. After we left her office, we drove just about one block, then turned right around and went back. Everyone in the office laughed and teased us as we had only been gone five minutes, and they told us they'd been expecting us. Thankfully the test was negative, and the rest is history.

AFTER 9/11, THE MEDIA WAS aware of Dan and me largely due to the article about us in the *New York Post*. And because of that, we have been privileged to have our stories told in several 9/11 books and two very important projects. The first of these was *Report from Ground Zero: The Story of the Rescue Efforts at the World Trade Center,* Dennis Smith's stunning account of the events of September 11 and their aftermath. It is the most gripping, accurate account of what happened through the eyes of the first responders, and also includes testimony from survivors, including me. Dennis is a retired member of the FDNY, and Dan met him very briefly in 1983, while at Ladder 38. I didn't meet him, though, until he interviewed us for the book. He is also an outstanding author who has written many other books, including *Report From Engine Co. 82* and *A Song For Mary.* ABC Television subsequently did a documentary based on Dennis' book, which we participated in, and which aired on September 10, 2002. We have since become friends with Dennis, and we are very thankful for the gift of his friendship.

Another project we were asked to be a part of was "Countdown To Ground Zero," which aired on The History Channel for the fifth anniversary of the attack. It was an Emmy-nominated documentary that retold several of that day's stories. One of them was the story of Jay Jonas, captain of Engine 9/Ladder 6 (now deputy fire chief). Jay and his crew were trying to make their way down a stairwell in the North Tower when the South Tower came down. He was certain the North Tower would soon follow. As they began making their descent they came upon a woman named Josephine on the twentieth floor. She had managed to make her way down from seventy-three, but was having difficulty at that point. Jay and his crew stopped to help her down, but doing that meant they had to move more slowly than they had before. Because of that, when the North Tower collapsed, rather than being near the ground floor, where they would probably have been killed, they were hunkered down in one of the stairwells that remained untouched, and survived. Josephine was the tool that Jesus used to save all of their lives, a true story of divine intervention. Miracles were all around that day, along with the pain, heartache, and despair.

Another story told in "Countdown to Ground Zero" was Rick Rescorla's. Rick was a retired army colonel, a veteran of combat in three wars, and, on 9/11, vice president of security for Morgan Stanley. Knowing about the attack on the World Trade Center in 1993, Rick's training, background, and foresight convinced him that the attackers would one day come back to finish things off. So he made sure his employees knew how to evacuate quickly. His dedication to his firm and the associates he worked with saved many of them that fateful day.

The documentary also highlighted the story of Brian Clarke and Stanley Praimnath. Brian was above the impact zone in the South Tower, and was descending when a group of women coming back up the stairs told him to go up to the roof rather than continue going down. All of a sudden he heard a man cry out for help. Making his way through the rubble and debris, he found Stanley and pulled him out. Despite the warning they'd received, they continued going down the stairs. Those who went up to the roof were killed. According to Stanley, "The Lord sent Brian as my guardian angel to help me that day." What a privilege it is for our story to be included along with these. We are truly humbled.

A LITTLE MORE THAN A year after we moved to Hemlock Farms, in June 2006, we were invited by QVC to participate in their twentieth anniversary Red Carpet Weekend. I was thrilled by the invitation, because living and working in New York City left little free time for shopping, and I had always found shopping with QVC to be extremely convenient. The pricing was also very competitive, and the quality of the merchandise superior. This event was a gathering of vendors and selected shoppers (like me), and took place at their headquarters in West Chester, Pennsylvania. As it turned out, it was one of the most magical experiences of my life. Oh, my goodness! Meeting the hosts was so much fun. And all of these terrific vendors under one roof!

One of the vendors whose booth we stopped at was Kirks Folly's, which makes whimsical costume jewelry and accessories. I had purchased my first Kirks Folly piece, a cherub pin with draped garnets, at Saks Fifth Avenue over twenty years ago. We were talking to Helen and Jenniefer Kirk, the founders, and I told them that when my Mitsy passed I wanted to put a necklace around her before we buried her. I'd first thought about a ruby heart Dan had given me, but then I chose one of my most treasured Kirks Folly pieces, "Secret of the Seven Angels." It was so beautiful—a long gold chain with seven angels and charms adorning it, each symbolizing different qualities. Every time I'd worn that necklace people had stopped me and complimented me on it. I loved it, and I knew my Mitsy would love it. So we buried her in my Kirks Folly angel necklace, angels to watch over her always, as she had watched over me. Jenniefer and Helen were completely overwhelmed by the story, as they are animal lovers and understood the significance of my gesture.

One thing led to another, and they discovered that Dan and I are 9/11 survivors. Helen, who is the designer, asked if I would help her design a piece of jewelry in honor of 9/11. After a number of emails back and forth between us, I suggested that, instead of a piece of jewelry, which would narrow the audience to women, she might make a wind chime. She liked my suggestion, and designed the most magnificent piece. I had suggested there be an angel somewhere in the piece, and she included a beautiful angel holding the earth, in the shape of a heart, in her arms. The angel sits atop large wings with a crystal heart in the center, with the chimes billowing down. The piece was entitled "To Remember," and it was completed and ready for shipment in September 2007. When it was ready to be presented on air, Jenniefer and Helen asked Dan and me to be their on-air guests. They introduced us and Jenniefer briefly told our story. It was quite an experience. And the piece was sold out by the next day. What an unbelievable experience, another part of God's plan! And what a privilege to work with the Kirk family and QVC!

DAN AND I ARE NOT the only people in Hemlock Farms who were touched by the tragedy of September 11. There are some who lost loved ones, and others whose loved ones survived. For example, one of our neighbors Fran and Pete Ferris' daughters-in-law was on the thirty-first floor in the North Tower and just made it out. At least partly because of that, Dan wanted to do something to help memorialize the day. Through Lee Ielpi, a highly-decorated retired firefighter who lost a son on 9/11, and who played an integral role in the search and rescue operation at Ground Zero, Dan was able to obtain a piece of World Trade Center steel to incorporate into a memorial in the community. And on September 11, 2007, he formally presented it to the community. The ceremony was attended by our World War Two veterans, our local police and fire departments, and many of our families. My stepson, Craig, came up to Hemlock Farms to help, and during the ceremony, he and I removed the bunting from the steel. It was so moving. Dan considers it a privilege to have obtained the steel for the community and to coordinate the memorial services. He feels it is the least he can do to make sure that no one ever forgets what happened that day.

CHAPTER SEVEN

Survivors

*For he shall give his angels charge over thee
to keep thee in all thy ways.*
Psalms 91:11

I RECENTLY WENT TO THE hospital with Dan when he had to undergo some tests, and when I mentioned to the nurse that we are survivors of 9/11, her jaw dropped, and she grabbed my hands and started rubbing them. And it wasn't the first time that happened. In fact, when people learn that we are survivors they often want to touch us. They also always ask the same two questions: "You were there that day?" and "What floor were you on?" I am an extremely touchy, feely kind of person, so I love it, but it is a bit perplexing. I'm astounded that people are so moved by the fact that we are survivors, even without knowing the depth of what we experienced.

It happened even when we met Susan Rescorla, who lost her beloved husband, Rick, on 9/11. Rick was a combat veteran of three wars, and the vice president of security for Morgan Stanley, whose quick thinking saved thousands of people that day. We met Susan during the preview of "Countdown to Ground Zero," which first aired on The History Channel for the fifth anniversary of 9/11. Much to my surprise, as soon as the preview was over, she grabbed my hands and started kissing them, saying, "God bless you." Thinking about it as I write this moves me to tears. Her husband was a hero, and yet she was moved by our story.

Of course, being a survivor, I wonder why Dan and I—as well as thousands of others—were spared on that fateful day. The only explanation I can offer is that it wasn't our time. But I also can't help thinking about those who didn't make it out of those buildings. I often wonder what their final thoughts were. How many of them, injured and in pain, had to face the realization that they wouldn't make it out? I know that people began jumping out of windows rather than endure the smothering heat and flames, and I am heartsick for all of these souls and their families. I was struck, when I read Chesley B. Sullenberger and Jeffrey Zazlow's *Highest Duty*—about the plane Sullenberger had to land in the Hudson River—that during the emergency air traffic control asked, "How many souls on board?" They didn't ask for the number of passengers and crew members. They asked for the number of souls. How brave were all of the souls that day on American Airlines 11 and United Airlines 175 which hit the World Trade Center, American Airlines 77 which hit the Pentagon, and United Airlines 93 which crashed in Shanksville, Pennsylvania? My heart weeps for all of them as well.

I have wondered, too, why so many suffered, so many lives were lost, and so many families were destroyed. I know that evil is never part of God's plan. But I also know in my heart that God, Jesus, and angel spirits were with all of those magnificent souls to ease their pain and suffering as they ascended into heaven. And I know, too, that Jesus continues to be with all of the families they left behind.

IN ONE WAY IT'S VERY easy to explain the effect that 9/11 had on us. Everything Dan and I had prior to that deadly day was taken away from us, everything, that is, except our lives. It's as if everything we knew before that day had vanished in the blink of an eye. Our home was no longer our home. Our careers would soon be over. And we lost so many friends and associates. But the loss was so great, and affected us in so many ways, that it's almost impossible to explain. For example, immediately after 9/11, I found that my brain seemed to be functioning at a much slower speed. It was very peculiar. I don't know if it was from the trauma, stress, shock, or some other reason, but my brain, normally very quick, was simply on "slow." And there wasn't anything I could do about it.

I also began to feel uncomfortable in Manhattan, even though by that time I had lived there for nine years. I remember walking down Fifth Avenue one day shortly after 9/11 and feeling like I was in some foreign country, as though everything in my world was gone, and being afraid that something horrible would happen. For the longest time I also had real discomfort whenever I was in a skyscraper. When I went back to work at Bank of America on West Fifty-Seventh Street, I was on an upper floor and it was very nerve-wracking. Of course, I wasn't the only one who felt that way. When Bank of America finally moved all its World Trade Center employees from the temporary offices in Secaucus, New Jersey, to West Thirty-Third Street, we asked to be put on a lower floor. In fact, it was only recently, when I attended several meetings at the National September 11 Memorial & Museum at the World Trade Center office, directly across from Ground Zero, that I realized that, by the grace of God, the skyscraper trauma seems to be gone.

I am still, though, very uncomfortable being anywhere that I can't exit quickly. If we go to a theater I always have to know where the nearest exit is, and I feel much more comfortable sitting close to it. That also means no planes for me. I was always a nervous flyer, but if I had to, I could get on one. I haven't been on a plane now since the spring of 2001, and I have no desire to. Immediately after 9/11, I got upset even when I could only hear a plane, much less see one. I'm okay with that now, but if a plane is flying close, like if we're near an airport and there's one right above us, I get very queasy. I even get queasy if I see the interior of a plane on TV or in the movies.

All of these things are symptoms of Post Traumatic Stress Disorder, and while it has gotten better over the years, it still rears its ugly head on occasion. Most of the time it's in the form of bad dreams. I'm not really sure what triggers these dreams, but the theme is almost always the same: No matter what I do, I can't seem to get home. I'm stuck in the city, either in a driving snow or rain storm, and I need to get a bus or some other form of transportation, and there are hundreds of people on line, and Dan is far away and I can't get to him. I also always have a sense that I'm in danger of being attacked by one or more people.

In one of the dreams I am in the lobby of a building in Battery Park City, the skies are as black as night, and there's a storm coming. Thunder, lightning, and I need to get home. Someone rolls down these iron windows to try and keep us safe, and I hear someone else saying something about protecting us from all the dead bodies on I-81 (which is nowhere near Manhattan). In another, I am somewhere in a commercial district with warehouses, and trying to get away from these roving gangs that are killing people with weapons of all kinds. There's a light bulb at the top of the staircase I'm hiding in, and the doors are locked. I know Dan is home, but I can't seem to get there.

But there are two dreams that are worse than any of the others. The first takes place at the Park Lane Hotel, while we are staying there. In the dream, I see a sharp shooter being lowered down in front of the hotel window. He's dressed all in black with a black mask, he aims his rifle at me, and just as he is about to shoot, I wake up. The other takes place in my childhood home in Brooklyn. There are bombs, explosions going off outside our home, and lots of smoke and fire—the Taliban are attacking and killing people, and I am hiding in my parents' living room, frozen with fear.

The dreams come much less frequently now than they used to, but they're not gone. I recently had a dream in which I am sitting by my jeep in Milford, Pennsylvania, a lovely town a few miles away from us, and a strange looking man with lots of jewelry on pulls out a gun. He starts coming after me, chasing me around my vehicle as I try hitting him with my bag. And in yet another dream, I am far from home attending a meeting, and all of a sudden an ice storm hits, and I can't get home. What am I going to do? The next thing I know I'm in a car with Dan driving back home. This is the first time that Dan appeared in one of my "I can't get home" dreams. I think it's a good sign.

By the Grace of God

ONE OF THE THINGS THAT helped Dan and me tremendously in our healing was that we experienced this horrific event together. They say the best thing for Post Traumatic Stress Disorder is "talk therapy," and we were each other's therapist. We could talk about what we experienced and what we were feeling with the knowledge that the other one understood completely. I'm sure that when other firemen who were fortunate enough to survive the day talked to their wives or families about what they went through, they received sympathy and compassion. But unless you were there you cannot relate to the magnitude and horror of it.

We were both an emotional mess, and it was particularly fortunate for us that we could turn to one another, because neither of us had the support of other survivors. Since I couldn't get out to Secaucus to work with my group, I didn't receive the counseling that my co-workers did. And even though Dan was with his brothers doing recovery work, he had been put on medical leave due to his injuries, so he wasn't at the firehouse. Looking back on it now, I know that was a blessing in disguise for him. The members of the FDNY were going through a very tough time, and I am grateful that he had to retire when he did. Difficult as retiring was for him, I think going back to work with so many of his brothers killed would have been truly devastating. Of course, to this day we still discuss the events of 9/11, and I'm so thankful that we had each other, that we got through the emotional trauma as a couple, and as individuals, and that we were brought to a wonderful new place and put on a new path.

SEPTEMBER 11 IS ALWAYS A very solemn day for us. As we approach the anniversary each year, it's as if some tremendous wave of grief and sorrow overtakes us. And every memory of that deadly day comes flooding back. We are very grateful for our blessings, but we are still heartbroken over the many who were lost. We remember those who perished, both those we knew and those we didn't, but I can't even begin to imagine the anguish that family members must feel when they remember their loved ones.

We often begin the day watching the names being recited on television. This is something that should be done every year, because people must never forget. The heartache is always there, it never goes away. Then we go to church, where we pray and light candles for all the mothers, fathers, sisters, brothers, wives, husbands, and children who were lost that day. It's never a day for small talk, and we try to avoid being around a lot of people, unless we attend a memorial service. For a couple of years Dan organized the memorial services in Hemlock Farms, but it was difficult for us because we would be separated all day. He would be at the firehouse preparing the service, and I would be home alone, and we wouldn't meet until around 7:00 PM for the memorial. So after two years he decided to let someone else handle the service so we would have enough time to be with our thoughts and honor all of those who were lost.

It only recently dawned on me that, ever since 9/11, I have been struggling to recreate what we lost that day. By the grace of God we survived, but nothing was the same afterward. My stepson uses the term "violently displaced," and that's a very accurate description. Living in Bronxville helped us start to heal, and moving to Pennsylvania has made an enormous difference. But even though I loved our home and my volunteer work, for a long time I felt that my life was somehow over, that I had no purpose. I had defined myself by what I did for a living. I had always worked, and I loved working, but when my career came to a screeching halt it was very difficult. I tried to get a part-time job, but there wasn't anything that really engaged my interest, and I became very frustrated. I wondered what I was supposed to be doing with my life, and struggled over it for a long time. And then, on April 10, 2009, someone suggested to me that I write this book. (As it happens, it was Good Friday, a very positive sign, I thought.) And then it all made sense. I must tell our story. I must share what Jesus did for us and continues to do for all of us. I must get His message out. My life is not over, it's just beginning.

ACKNOWLEDGEMENTS

I would like to thank Rob Kaplan for his heartfelt dedication to this project. Rob has truly captured the essence of what Dan and I went through, as well as capturing what was in my heart and what I wanted to convey. Without Rob, this book would not have been published.

I would also like to thank my wonderful parents, Amy and John, whose unwavering love and support have been with me always; my stepson, Craig, who continues to be an inspiration to me every day; my sweet brother, John, who is with me always; and my wonderful husband, Dan, whose love and continued support I treasure. He was my rock during this process, and also made sure this would come to fruition.

There are many people in the pages of this book whose love and friendship I am so grateful for, and I thank them all from the bottom of my heart. And of course, Jesus, for without him, we wouldn't be here today.

JEAN POTTER IS A NATIVE of Brooklyn, New York. Retired from her position at Bank of America, she and her husband, Dan, a retired New York City fireman, now live in Lords Valley, Pennsylvania, where they devote their time to volunteer activities and their families.

ROB KAPLAN IS THE EDITOR, author, or co-author of several books in a variety of fields, including *A Passion for Books* (with Harold Rabinowitz), *Strategic Negotiation* (with Brian J. Dietmeyer), and *Helping the Addict You Love* by Lawrence Westreich, M.D. He lives in Cortlandt Manor, New York.